MW00655205

A Gold Digger's Guide

DISCLAIMER: Though the term Gold Digger is used on the cover of this book, from here on out, get accustomed to the New Millennium term: GOAL Digger. It's about achieving GOALs.

DO NOT

GET CAUGHT

WITH THIS

BOOK!

A Gold Digger's Guide

*How to Get What You Want,
Without Giving It Up.*

By: Baje Fletcher

GLITZ & GLAMOUR PUBLISHING

Edited by Mila Hiles and Tosha Boyd

The names of the characters identified in this book have been modified or changed completely to avoid litigation.

PRINTED IN THE UNITED STATES OF AMERICA

Visit the website: www.AGoldDiggersGuide.com for more information on products, projects or the author.

Interior book design by Cadillac. Exterior book design by Blacktag Media. Logo design by Mark Merit. Front cover photo by Le Mar James. Back cover photo by Facet Photography. Makeup on front cover by Chantel Mckinney. Makeup on back cover by Red Star. Dress on back cover designed by Danielle Kelly.

ISBN# 978-0-615-24824-0

To Mums:
Thank you for giving my life purpose and meaning.

This book is dedicated to Demiqua, Danielle, and
all women who need some motivation and guidance.

Table of Contents

Acknowledgements

First of all, I want to thank God who has pulled me through so many situations that could have broken me down, some of which my closest friends know nothing about. Secondly, to my grandmother Syble Dixon, I want to thank you for instilling strength in me. As a teen I could not understand your way of doing things but now as a woman I realize that you only tried to protect me and steer me in the right direction. Your tough love made me a self-sufficient individual woman. I spent more time with you than I did with my own parents; you are and will always be my backbone. Since I began writing this book you passed on but you will never be forgotten. You are cherished.

To my parents, life doesn't always go according to plan but I know that you both did your best. Daddy, I was such a rebellious teen, it's amazing how forgiving you are. Now that I'm a woman with responsibilities of my own, I learned to truly appreciate the sacrifices you made. I love you. Mom, you're no longer here physically, but I know you're here in spirit. I will never meet another woman so ladylike and so humble. You are deeply missed, but I know you're in a better place.

Mr. James Cannon (*my mentor*), you came into my life when I needed someone to cheer me on. This book was merely an idea but because of your constant motivation and encouragement, what began only as an idea is now a product. Thank you for believing in me just as much as I believe in myself. I can still hear you say, "You can do it Sweetie!"

Annetta Bryant, since the moment we met I've been drawn to you as if you were a missing piece of my life. You took me under your wings and gave me strength and guidance when I needed it the most. You are such a nurturer. I got accustomed to making my own decisions and fending for myself so it was a huge relief to have you to help steer my life. You are like a mother to me.

To the most important person in my life, *I call you "Mums."* We met for the first time four years ago and you changed me for the better. Because of you my life has meaning. Your photo lives in a lavender frame on the nightstand by my bed; it's the last thing I see when I go to sleep and the first thing I see when I wake. It keeps me strong and focused, and is a constant reminder that failure is not an option. I have to make sacrifices now because I can see the bigger picture but never doubt how much I love you.

Special thanks to Johnny Mack (*Writer for the Stars*) and Kwaku Agyapong Jr. (*President of BajeFanClub.com*) for your coaching, advice and male perspective. Thanks to Noble Coban (*Manager*), Lemar J (*photographer*), Mike McKoy & Ahmed Almodovar (*Marketing Team*) and David Hawkins (*Bodyguard/Chauffeur*) for your services, guidance and constant motivation because I couldn't have carried out this task efficiently without you all.

If I had to list some of you by name it would be a page long. *What the heck...you all deserve it.* Thanks to Jinae Monroe, Debby St. Louis, Able Hernandez, Craig Alan, Willet, Una, Herman, Hayworth, Tony, Jermain, Jacqueline, Justin, Alma Fletcher, Keisha Robb, Joanne Theodule, Tasha Williams, Bryant Aleem, Alonzo Phillips, Magic City, Andy Holguin, Dexter Murray, Michael Donaldson, Yami De Jesus, Van Silk, Tony Wilkins, Roger Stone, Nasheka Harper, Chris Phashion, Rasheed Jones, Biz, Tony Mateo, Paulemele, Sophia Jones, Pablo Who, Sean Cummings, Paris Hilton, E40, Carl, Conroy Thomas, Calvin Mignott, Evens St. Preux,

Kevin Watson, Benji Brown, Tight Mike, Haitian Fresh, K Slay, SBK, Yvone Banton, Angela, Tony Mateo, Melisa Morrison, Rose Lewis, Marcha Thompson, Shayla, Donna, Davon Crawford, June Gooden, Evans Starke, Simply Jess, Craig Huey, Richard Franklin, BeBe, Emerson Lopez, Wayne Freeman, Ezra Masters, Leo Marshal, Larry Mace, Lee Nelson, Paula Benjamin, Arthur Braddy III, Bridget Butler, Horace Madison, Robert Clark, Anthony Allen, Anthony Truss, Michelle Myers, Eric Touzalin, Miss Ena, Shirley, Sonia, Betty, Alex Burns and all those who I've met along the way who've allowed me to let my voice be heard, lightened my load by lending me money, giving me a helping hand, a shoulder to cry on, words of encouragement and even a place to lay my head. Because of what you all have done for me I have a weakness for helping the underdog, (including battered women, the homeless and foster kids). Thanks for all who believed in me and shared my vision, especially with this book.

Introduction

...Life Lessons

You have the power inside to live life as you see fit. Don't allow anyone to take that God-given right from you. No amount of money, fame, or prestige is worth a life lived only to please others. You are the ultimate answer on right and wrong for yourself.

About two years ago I came across a "tell-all" book that caught my attention. It was about a woman who resorted to having sex with guys to make ends meet. This story stunned the world because all the subjects she wrote about were high-profile celebrities. Her story disturbed me as it did everyone who read it, but it weighed on my mind for another reason. I wasn't so much stunned as I was saddened. I was sad because the life she lived isn't as uncommon as the world thinks it is. The entertainment industry moves at an accelerated speed. Beautiful women are a dime a dozen and celebrities have money to buy whatever or whomever they want; the outcome can be devastating. The effects are intensified when judgment becomes cloudy because drugs and alcohol are added to the mix. The only thing uncommon about her story was that her subjects were all people that we knew and loved. The truth is, there are many more women with similar stories – *maybe on a smaller scale, but nevertheless similar.*

There are a lot of women (young and old) who don't know their self-worth. How could they when statistics show that at least 50% of marriages result in divorce and a great deal of children end up being raised in a dysfunctional or a single-parent home? We have seen the effects on society from boys who were raised without fathers, but what about the girls? When there is no male present in the household, who preps her for what's to be expected from the opposite sex and who teaches her "the game" from a male's point of view? Who will set the bar high by being the example of how she should be treated?

In my interviews with women, I've discovered that in 80% of homes where fathers were present, there was also an invisible barrier that prohibited him from talking to his daughter about sex. I'm not just talking about elementary sex education. Girls need to know the emotional damage that may lie ahead by giving themselves to someone undeserving, so it's pertinent that they be taught what type of guys to avoid. Young women need to know what behaviors are expected from "players" so when presented to them, women can not only recognize them, but avoid them. Someone needs to show them how to plan ahead, so if they're ever in a compromising situation they don't just respond, but instead react efficiently. Some would say that most parents have failed, if you disagree then take a look at the rate of teenage pregnancies, abortions, single moms on welfare and the overwhelming rate of STDs. Unfortunately, because of AIDS, you can lose just one round and be put out of the game...for life.

We as women sometimes sell ourselves short. We know that he hardly ever calls, and when he does it's late at night; yet we accept the lies or make excuses for him while we look the other way. We sometimes put up with so much and give too much of ourselves to the wrong people because we are trying to fill a void within. Some of us are so afraid of being alone that we'd rather have anyone in our lives, even if they're pessimistic, emotionally exhausting or abusive. Some of us have allowed our self esteem to be beaten so low that we think we don't deserve the good things that come our way; I've heard many cases of women substituting Hallmark cards with their bodies. I spoke with numerous women who admitted to having sex with guys - not because they loved them, not because they're attracted to them, but because they felt obligated because the guy paid a bill or bought them something nice. [Reluctantly] *"Girl, he paid my car note this month, so now I'm going to have to give him some."* What part of the game is that? Whatever happened to a "thank you" card?!

It's time we stop going along with the flow. No more hanging on for the ride, it's time we grab a hold of the wheel and steer our own lives. We must map out the route and decide our destination. In all aspects of life: we can't just accept what we're given if we're not satisfied with it, and no more "putting out" because of guilt. A lot of us don't realize our potential or the **power** that we possess. In a nation where women are allowed to do amazing things like vote, voice opinions, and have equal opportunities in the workforce, there is no excuse to use sex as barter. A man can earn the money that he gave to us back, but we can't get back the part of us that we gave to him. We are precious, we deserve the best, and we have the **power**. We shouldn't be tempted to break our rules or bend our standards because we don't have to. *We don't have to have sex to be sexy; our sexual essence is more than enough.*

We have the greatest thing that men want unless they're homosexuals. Even then, a lot of them try to imitate your feminine essence. Men work on our terms and on our time. Never forget that. Most of them will do anything for *IT.* How many guys have lost their best friend because they lived out a scene from the movie "The Best Man"? *You know the scene I'm talking about:* when Morris Chestnut (the groom) beat up Taye Diggs (his best man) because he found out that Taye slept with his fiancée. Mythical or not, one of the greatest wars between two nations was because of a woman (Helen of Troy), and even the Bible showed us the **power** that Eve had over Adam. Many politicians have fell victim to call girls and even interns. Many guys have gone broke because of the "booby trap" (strip club) and countless fellows have lost their wives, careers, and their freedom. You didn't make them the way they are, but by analyzing them you can capitalize. Physically we aren't stronger than them, but we don't have to be because we were born with built-in artillery; we possess the art of seduction. Yes, we can weaken them with our curves, our words, but the effects last longer when we do so with our minds. *Plan ahead, do your research and follow through.* Getting their financial favors for sex is easy, getting them without having to give up anything? Now that's the challenge.

When I first disclosed the idea of writing this book, I was alarmed at how many people asked me if it would be a "tell-all" because that simply isn't my forte. I don't want to be a successful author if it means putting everyone's business and inner-most secrets out there. Betrayal and breaking up homes aren't options for me. My passion for writing this book is so that women can benefit from the shortcuts I've discovered and even my very own shortcomings.

IN THIS BOOK I'LL COVER:

The Wish List
Ways to Make $
Golden Occupations
Simple Makeover Tips
Looking in the Right Places
Subjects to Get Educated In
The Ten Steps to Success

How to Dig Safely
How to Stand Out
How to Get In VIP with Ease
How to Delay the Sex Discussion
How to Administer the "Cheap Test"
How to Memorize His Phone Number

"Friday" Technique
"Subliminal" Technique
"Double Up" Technique
"Teamwork" Technique
"Identifying" Technique
"Stick & Go" Technique
"Categorizing" Technique
"Invest in Self" Technique
"Dumb Down" Technique
"Island Hopping" Techniques

And many more shortcuts to getting what you want.

THE FOLLOWING CHAPTER COVERS:

Webster's Dictionary definition of Gold Digger

Baje's definition of a Gold Digger

Baje's definition of a GOAL Digger

"Categorizing" Technique

SECTION: I

Change Your Mindset

Chapter 1

KNOW WHAT YOU WANT

...Knowing is Half the Battle.

Knowing what you want is a very important lesson because it will direct you where to look and determine what it is exactly that you are seeking.

Not so fast…
If you skipped over the introduction, please
go back and read it thoroughly.

Know What You Want

Heed the wisdom that others have poured into you. You can save yourself time, energy and heartbreaks if you listen to others and learn from their mistakes.

With a combination of experiences, instincts, and street smarts, you can be a step ahead of the game. So read and learn. Some things you may or may not agree with. Use what you need and leave what you don't. When you finish reading, I hope you feel that you have gained some useful knowledge that you can use in your everyday life. Go get it girl!

Life is about challenging yourself and going after the things that most people only dream about, whether they are materialistic or personal achievements. *You live life to the fullest when you realize that it's not about settling, but rather constantly setting GOALs and pursuing them.* My GOAL is to empower and encourage you. It is possible to obtain all that you want, but you have to be focused and never lose sight of yourself. When you know who you are, you are not easily swayed.

You can get what you want and be what you want without sacrificing your body. This book is about accomplishing your GOALs without compromising. It's about maximizing your potential, embracing your confidence, and owning your **power**.

What is your ultimate life GOAL?

_____

_____

_____

_____

_____

_____

_____

_____

_____

_____

_____

_____

_____

Is your immediate GOAL to get married? If so, you just bought the wrong book Honey! This book isn't about waiting for Prince Charming to come and rescue you. It's about rescuing yourself, by recognizing opportunities, and thinking outside the box, so ultimately you'll be able to pave your own way. It's time to command CHANGE. No more settling, no more accepting the crumbs we're given. I wrote this book for women who are tired of seeing guys walking around with their chests puffed out high as if they are the boss of us. Tired of seeing guys rub their hands together when they talk and give the nod from across the room like they're some sort of players. The type of guy who will throw a couple of dollars in the air claiming to "make it rain," just to get satisfaction from seeing women, *I mean girls,* scrambling on the floor to pick up singles. These players think they're so smooth and just know they have us all figured out. Well, the tables have turned! *Welcome to the new millennium.*

Webster's Dictionary Definition of Gold Digger:

Part of Speech: *noun* **Definition:** opportunist **Synonyms:** bloodsucker, exploiter, leech, parasite, sponge, user; also known as a woman who associates with or marries a rich man in order to get valuables from him through gifts or a divorce settlement.

Baje's definition of Gold Digger:

Gold Digger is a phrase coined by guys and used as a method of reverse psychology on women. However, women also use it against each other in hopes of keeping the other down. A term created so women expect less from the male species and experience episodes called: "guilt trips" if they dare suggest that anything related to finances is expected from the opposite sex; a derogatory term which many women have bought into and been bounded by…until now.

Baje's definition of GOAL Digger:

A GOAL Digger is a female that utilizes her surroundings to the maximum to achieve her GOALs and better her life.

A GOAL Digger is an individual who knows what she wants out of life and isn't afraid to think and step out of the box to make her dreams into a reality. She's a risk-taker. A focused, self-sufficient, self-driven, and GOAL-oriented individual who is committed to success and accepts that failure is simply not an option. A woman who will not fall for "game" and won't hesitate to utilize those suspected of being a hindrance to the GOALs that have been set.

…I Have a Dream

You have a dream. It's been planted in your mind for years now. Hopefully it's deeper than obtaining materialistic things. Maybe it's making your voice heard, helping others, teaching others, or providing for your family. Whatever it is, the time to bring that dream to reality is NOW. You live only once. Live your life fully by embracing your GOALs and going after them. Our dreams are what separate us from the next individual, but most people don't have the fortitude to go against societal norms. The few who were strong enough to do so were the ones who made it in the Hall of Fame, became Stars, Icons, Idols, Leaders and Presidents. Don't allow non-believers and dream-killers to stop you from claiming the life that you are destined to have. You are a dreamer like me, I believe in you.

I summed up my experiences, and the advice of others that I've met along the way who wanted to see me succeed. I want to be in your corner cheering you on the way those close to me cheered for me. I'm providing you all the secrets I discovered, saving you time and heartbreaks so that you can get to your financial destination in half the time that I did. So before you turn another page, get a sheet of paper and a pen because it's time to start planning your future. As you read, write down the most important points to you so that you don't forget them.

One day I made a promise to never settle for less than I deserve and I kept that promise.

What's Your Promise to Yourself?

_____
_____
_____
_____
_____
_____
_____
_____
_____
_____
_____
_____
_____
_____
_____

"If you stand for nothing, you will fall for anything."

<u>Lesson: #1.</u> *All money isn't good money.   If a guy will give you money but you are sure that he's the type to "kiss and tell," then don't even deal with him.*

If he will discuss with others what he has done to you, or for you, then he's just not worth your time. You don't want a guy like that because other people will know your tactics and your strategies may become less effective. In other words: it can kill your game if your angle is already anticipated.

There are too many women "screwing" their way to nowhere. If a guy is that much of a low life that he requires you to sleep with him before he works with you, then who is to say that he will keep up his part of the bargain after? I feel obligated to share with women some of my experiences (both good and bad) so they can guard themselves against making life-altering mistakes.

Lesson: #2. *Dropping hints only works 20% of the time.*

When I was young, I had a naïve way of thinking so I dropped hints around guys. I said that my hair was a mess or I would let them know I couldn't talk on my cell phone too long because I was over my minutes. I found that 80% of the time that approach didn't work. It just left me feeling frustrated because I realized that most guys are cheap by nature. They would pretend not to hear my comments because they really didn't care anyway! Now I flat out ask for what I want. If my request is denied, I simply leave right then and there. I leave just after I delete their number from my phone (right in front of them) or I give them back their business card. *Once a number is deleted, there isn't a darn thing they can do to get it back in.* The important thing is that I don't get upset, because I know that I saved myself the guessing work. I get straight to the point so I don't waste my valuable time. After all, time is money.

Lesson: #3. *If it is difficult for you to ask for something, there are two great inventions called email and text messaging.*

To get the best results, I'd suggest asking face to face. It will be even harder for him to tell you "no" if you are in public, so don't be too shy to ask him for things in the presence of other people. If you decide to ask through a text message, then send him a sexy picture mail right before you pop the question and watch how the likelihood of him giving you what you want shoots through the roof. *Just make sure it's not a nude or incriminating photo.*

Once you ask for what you want, most guys will grant you your wish (if they have it within their budget). You may ask why that is. It is because they want what you have and if they tell you "no" then there is a big chance that they won't get it. Telling you "no" would mean that all the money they spent on dinners, movies and courting you in general would have been for nothing (so that isn't a smart move). Over the years, I found out that it was the broke guys that would ask questions like: "I just met you and you want me to take you shopping?" Yet it would never be too early for them to sleep with you, right?

Guys aren't mind readers. When you start telling them what you need and start asking for what you want, you'll be surprised at how much you're able to get out of them. There is a technique that I'd suggest you use when asking for things because even though most guys have one-track minds and are easy to figure out, they often fall into the following categories.

"CATEGORIZING" TECHNIQUE

Lesson: #4. *If you use the wrong technique on the wrong man, you will get nothing, so make sure you categorize them correctly.*

Type A

Most guys fall under Type A (**Joe Shmo**). Most Type A's have been in a few relationships and may have been burned previously. As a result, some are extremely cautious about giving money to a woman in fear that she may run off soon after. In addition, most Type A's are average fellows that work nine-to-five jobs and may be living from paycheck to paycheck. Chances are he's not going to be able to give you the full amount you request. So in order to get the amount you desire, you'll have to ask at least three more guys also. If you did your research thoroughly and selected the right individuals, between all four guys you should meet your GOAL. With this type you can flat out say something along the lines of: your rent is due on the first of the month, it is $800, and you need help paying it, can he help you. Even though it's direct, you still want to leave him with some dignity, so don't be rude about it. The bad news is that with a Type A fellow, there is a only a 30/70 chance of getting what you want, because even though he may want to contribute to your cause, his fears and finances just may not allow him to. The good news is the sooner you ask him for something is the sooner you'll see if he's in the 30% or 70% and you can evaluate the situation more proficiently.

Type B

Type B (**Captain Save-a-"Ho"**). Most type B's are older, some even retired. This type of guy wants to feel like he is needed and has a purpose in life. He may be a guy that is longing for a family, but he has no children of his own or a guy who has succeeded in most aspects of his life and is now looking for a new "project." You can say something along the lines of: it's so embarrassing that you even have to ask for a favor of this magnitude because you are so independent, but this month you ran into some unexpected things and can't afford to pay the rent. Tell him that you waited to the last minute to even mention it because you thought you would have figured out a way by now and is there any way he could possibly help you. As soon as he agrees to give you what you asked for, make sure to start smiling - because smiles and giggles is what this type thrives on. With a Type B fellow, there is an 80/20 chance of getting what you want, because he feels the need to rescue the damsel in distress. The good news is this type has a tendency to keep commitments, so if he agreed to do something for you, he more than likely will. If you have a problem with middle-aged men, then the bad news is he'll probably be considerably older than you.

Type C

Type C (**The Sucker**). A *Sucker* can come in any age range or income bracket. He yearns for a woman's attention, whether it's good or bad; for some odd reason he works better under pressure and doesn't mind being told what to do. Maybe he was a late bloomer and the girls rarely paid him attention, maybe he has a lot of siblings and didn't get enough attention as a child. Most Type C's have just been through a divorce or are in the process of getting one. You'll more than likely find this type of fellow in a place where he has to pay for some attention like a strip club. *FYI: Most strip clubs don't allow women entrance unless they're accompanied by a male, because most women don't tip other women. So if you plan on scouting at a strip-club then bring one of your male friends to tag along.* With Type C, simply say something along the lines of: this is my life, and I choose to live it the way I want to. If you aren't doing something to make my life better then you're simply making it worse. I have no patience for cheapness, so if you don't give me what I want, then the next guy will. My rent is due today. Are you going pay it or not? When you come across a Type C, never make him feel like he is in control by asking for his permission; just tell him what you want. Out of all the types listed, this one is set in his ways the most (which is a good thing for you). More good news is with a Type C fellow there is a 90/10 chance of getting what you want. The bad news is that most wealthy men don't fall in this category, because it's impossible to accumulate and maintain wealth by being a *Sucker*.

Type D

Type D (**The Dic-tator**). Only 5% of guys fall under this category. Usually Type D's have money and have decided to set up a defense mechanism to protect it. Most Type D's have been divorced…without a prenuptial agreement…that is. Type D's are all about independent women. With Type D's, the woman who asks for something gets nothing, and the woman who asks for nothing gets everything. With this type, just know that you're not going to get anything overnight; you're going to have to be in it for the long haul. If you are willing to dedicate some time to work on Type D, then set a time limit prior. If you haven't met your GOAL by your deadline then you have to be strong enough to walk away. *You are in a world of trouble if you mistake a Type E for a Type D.*

Type E

Type E (**The Con-Artist**). A man who reads this book and is trying to outsmart you by telling you he's Type D (so that you don't ask him for anything).

*None of the types listed is permanent. Just because a guy is Type A today doesn't mean he can't go from A to D in a few months or years. Types can change drastically with a pay raise or promotion. So it's important that you constantly assess your target. **Note:** Others may fall into categories that aren't listed above. If you come across a guy with a hustler's mentality or if he's on top of his game and knows your motives, then there is no use to butt heads. Just quietly move along to the next target.*

... Learn to get straight to the point

Frankly, I am tired of the repetitive dinner and the movies thing. So the worst thing that a Penny Pincher can ask me is: what do I want to do. It will be a loss for him because my answer will be:

"I want to go shopping."

Good luck to him trying to see me a second time if he dare says "no." There are more important things that I could be doing, like working on somebody else or catching up on sleep. Numerous times I've been asked:

"So in order for a guy to get with you, he has to spend money on you?"

And my answer will always be:

"I'm not for sale."

Because I know that he'll spend his money on me and still get nothing in return.

Lesson: #5. _Never apologize or justify anything._ **_When he sees you as more of an authority figure, he'll be more compelled to give you what you want without asking questions or second-guessing you._**

Every time you say you are sorry, you hand over your **power**. If you arrived late, there is no need for apologies because he's lucky that you showed up in the first place. Don't forget to mention how busy you were and how much you had to put aside to meet with him. *Guys feel so special when they think you put time aside just for them.* If you quoted him a price for an item and when you both got to the store it was more than you expected, it's not your fault. If he went behind your back and tried to gather information about you and found out something that he didn't want to hear, you still don't owe him an apology because he should have been respecting your privacy in the first place. Never let him forget that. The usual "I'm a grown woman" response usually puts him back in his place. Training him should start early. You can't hesitate to put him back in line the second he steps out otherwise he'll continue to test the limits. You shouldn't feel bad about putting him in the doghouse when he messes up, because he will be more willing to over compensate with gifts when he is feeling guilty. Do not be afraid to send him to voicemail, or say that you are tied up at the moment, and you'll call him later. Let him marinate and think of ways he can buy his way back in. Guys are never too old for a time out (T.O).

THE NEXT CHAPTER COVERS:

"Double Up" Technique

"Stick & Go" Technique

"Invest in Self" Technique

"Teamwork" Technique

"Island Hopping" Techniques

The Wish List

Chapter 2

MAKE A WISH LIST

...Naughty Is In, Nice Is Out.

All items on your *Wish List* must translate into GOALs. These items should only be tools that will aid you and your loved ones in achieving the ultimate GOAL - a self-sufficient lifestyle (financial freedom).

Make a Wish List

Write down all the things that you want- necessities first. It may be as small as your monthly bills. Make sure to prioritize and itemize your expenses because soon you'll have to match the item up to the man. Don't be apprehensive to ask for the pricier items even if you think that he cannot afford it because you may be pleasantly surprised. *"Shoot for the moon and if you fall short you'll land among the stars."*

"DOUBLE UP" TECHNIQUE

This technique is an easy one, once it's introduced to you. Always ask for more than you need, because chances are he's going to try to negotiate with you. If you need $1 to buy something, tell him it cost $2 because he'll more than likely say that he can only afford $1…perfect. It is a win-win situation (for you anyway).

I actually discovered it on accident. I had a Sugar Daddy (SD) a few years ago. Everything I asked him for I got…he even had my bank account number programmed in his PDA so it was on hand whenever he needed to wire me money. He was such a good boy. Then all of a sudden I noticed a change in his behavior. Whenever I would tell him that I wanted something, he would tell me that he could only come up with about half of what I asked for; I quickly found a solution for that problem. I started *doubling up*. So if something cost $450, I would simply tell him it cost $900. When he took me shopping, the cashiers in the stores had jealousy written all over their faces. I remember on one of our shopping sprees while I was trying on outfits in the fitting room I overheard one of the store employees talking to him. When I got out of the fitting room, I asked him what they were discussing. He said that she asked him if I was his daughter or were we related. I guess she was shocked to see him spending all that money on a woman half his age. When I was ready to cash out I told her that he was my daddy, Sugar Daddy that is. I smiled at her, grabbed my bags, and went on my way.

"STICK & GO" TECHNIQUE

Lesson: #6. *Avoid promises at all costs. A promise is a technique that guys use to ensure you'll stick around.*

Let's not get greedy; you have to know when to stop otherwise you'll fall into the Carrot Trap. It's like dangling a carrot in front of a donkey so it will keep walking. Do NOT fall for that! If you do, then you are sure to end up getting screwed...literally. Tell him that the future isn't promised so you live for *now*. Get one thing on your list, cross it off and do the "Slip-a-Roo" (move on). Give yourself bonus points if you kill more than one bird with one stone, but I highly recommend to never stick around for item number two because *if he really wants to give you a present, there's no time like the present.*

Create a short-term and a long-term list. The short-term list would probably be the newest palm pilot that's out or your expenses for that month. The long-term list would probably be paying off college, getting the down payment for a house, or even hitting the goldmine (paying it off completely). We live in a world where the possibilities are endless, so aim high. Do not underestimate **The Power of the PEN**. Write down everything that you want on a sheet of paper and post it up in your home so you're constantly reminded of your GOALs. If you're very ambitious you may need a few sheets. Before you know it, you will have crossed off all your items on the list. Ladies be careful though, one time I left my list laying around and a guy that liked me saw it. Listed on it were all of all the things I wanted from guys, including him. He picked it up and asked: "Who is this for, Santa Claus?" Good thing his name wasn't on it.

<u>Lesson: #7.</u> Make sure that all the items on your list are essential in accomplishing your GOALs, so you'll be able to continue making money after you give him the boot.

"INVEST IN SELF" TECHNIQUE

<u>Lesson: #8.</u> By having expensive or expensive looking items, you attract an expensive crowd.

A laptop would be an ideal item for your list because you can use it for work or school. Even better, have him pay for some of your college classes or pay for you to learn a trade (that way you can secure a decent career and make your own money even after he's no longer in the picture). If you are a make-up artist, have him take you on a shopping spree at the make-up store because you can always do makeovers for other people and get paid. I won't scrutinize you for a few brand-name items, because unfortunately we live in a world where you are judged by how you look, what you drive and what you wear. In doing so, it's important to not go overboard and remember that purses, cars, and shoes are not the GOALs. They are only tools of the trade that will aid in getting you closer to your GOAL; they don't have to be the newest models or the latest editions, just something shiny, slick or bold enough to make a statement will do because they depreciate. Make sure they don't become habit forming collector items because they're considered liabilities, not assets. *I'll explain the difference in Chapter Nine.*

"TEAMWORK" TECHNIQUE

Some women don't want to help each other out for fear that the other woman might outshine them, but if we all work together then we all can accomplish more. Two shovels are better than one. We just have to remember to help those who helped us out.

Lesson: #9. If you have a girlfriend that is also a go-getter then you both may be able to work together, so compare notes and exchange ideas.

It was early March, and just a day or two before my birthday when my best friend Chelli and I decided to go to the boutiques downtown. We were walking in the shopping district when my eyes caught a baby pink hand-knitted dress so we decided to go in the store for a closer look. I tried the dress on, it fell right above my knees, it had a low cut back and it hugged my body perfectly…it seemed as if it was made just for me. I didn't want to take it off but neither did I want to spend $500. Reluctantly I took it off, but I had a plan. As we left the store I told the flamboyant cashier that I was going to find a guy to pay for it and I'd be back soon. He winked his left eye, snapped his fingers and said,

"I know you will."

About five minutes later after stepping out of the store we walked past a chain of restaurants and were approached by two guys. I quietly whispered to Chelli to keep walking because those guys looked like they didn't have any money (*they both looked like thugs, they wore their pants extra baggy and one even had gold teeth*). The first thing they asked us was if we wanted to grab a bite to eat. It's not like we were on a time schedule, so we took them up on the offer - just so we could kill some time until some bigger fish came along. Just as we finished our margaritas and lobster, Chelli opened the "digging" conversation like we planned and done so many times before. She said,

"Baje, you should get that dress you tried on for your birthday".

I responded,

"Girl, I'm not supposed to buy my *own* birthday gift."

Immediately one of the guys butted in, he asked how much the dress cost and I told him $500. I thought that he was going to change the subject from that point on but to my surprise he didn't. The next thing he said was:

"Let's go get it."

Lesson: #10. Collaborate with people behind the scenes like store clerks. They're the last people that your target will think are on your side.

We went back to the store and he purchased the dress for me. The flamboyant cashier quickly brought some shoes for me to try on also and they were absolutely hideous. When I told him that I didn't like them he whispered in my ear,

"Girl, you don't have to, just have him pay for them and then return it when he's gone and we can split the money."

And so we did. Chelli and I kept in contact with our new found friends, because we knew that they'd come in handy from time to time.

"ISLAND HOPPING" TECHNIQUES

Make sure to put all the countries that you want to visit on your list because it is very much possible to get to all of them without you having to pay for any of the trips.

A. One way that you can travel without having to pay for it is by signing up for frequent flyer miles with the airline of your choice and eventually you'll incur enough to earn free flights. You can even have your friends and associates donate the miles that they earned from previous flights to you.

B.   The easiest way to meet foreigners is to scout tourist spots and attractions like theme parks because if you and a target get along, he may be willing to fly you to his country in order to see you again.

C.   Don't rule out the ESL (English as a second language) and foreign exchange students due to their lack of English skills, because they too can come in handy; when they're going back home for the holidays that may very well be your free ticket to a country on your *Wish List.   So make a mental note that foreign accents are a very good thing.*

D.   Another way to get a free trip is to find a guy who travels a lot, he may be happy to fly you out to the next city or country that he has to go to for business.   So the next time you are in the airport take a minute to look at the flight information screens to see if there are flights going to one of the places on your *Wish List.*   Find out what gate number that plane takes off from and hang out in that section for a few minutes.   You may meet someone that is willing to take you there.

E.   Airport employees are likely to travel often, and they get big discounts and perks when they do so.   Once airport personnel add you to their benefits, you can fly for free and in most cases they're unable to remove your name for one whole year *(so work it, work it).*

F.   Cruises are awesome!   You'll get more for HIS money. For one price you get all you can eat, live entertainment, Vegas-style shows, planned activities, games, plus you can club hop.   The best thing of all is that the ship is so big that it will be super easy to ditch him.

Do your research ahead of time and also buy a map of the country you plan on visiting and a language translation book- in the event that it isn't an English-speaking country. You may even want to sign up on social sites like Hyves.com to try to meet other fellows while you are there also, just in case your guy decides to act up. *This also applies to state-to-state travel.* Always call someone you know in the state/country that you are traveling to ahead of time and let them know you'll be in their area in the event that things don't go according to plan. **Note:** Use caution while using social sites. You wouldn't give someone your phone number after just meeting them right? So, the same screening process applies.

You can apply the *Double Up* technique to traveling also by taking the following into consideration. When a guy flies you somewhere, tell him to purchase you a first-class seat. Let's say the first-class seat costs $800 and the coach seat costs $400. Once he purchases the first class seat, call the airline and change it to a coach seat. Now you'll have $400 left over. If he used his credit card you won't be able to get the cash back but you can get a voucher and use it toward a future flight, which is just as good.

The second way you can double up on trips is by having your target fly one of your girlfriends out with you also. One guy that likes me happens to be in a line of work that requires him to fly to a different country every week. If he wants me to meet him there, I'll tell him not only to fly me but also a girlfriend of mine there a few days before he gets in so we can mingle, go to the beach and do girl stuff until he comes. A few years ago he flew my girlfriend Audrey and me to Jamaica. We climbed Dunn's River Falls- it's one of the major tourist spots in Ocho Rios. We also partied at

"Jamaican Me Crazy" nightclub in the Jamaica Grande Resort. *What happens in Jamaica stays in Jamaica.*

Dunn's River Falls in Ocho Rios, Jamaica

Nassau Bahamas   Photos by: Johnathan Simms

THE WISH LIST

Some people have different names for it like: focal, GOAL or vision board…I call it the *Wish List*. Listed on it are items I want, places I want to go, people I want to meet and bills I need to pay off. Most importantly, GOALs I want to accomplish, and steps and strategies to get to those people, places and GOALs are also listed. Sure some of the things are farfetched, but they're supposed to be. I created the list to keep me focused, keep me striving, to push me to my maximum potential.

When I was about twenty years old I made my first *Wish List* and an associate of mine saw it. Listed on it were all the items I wanted, things I wanted to accomplish, and (at that particular time) a lot of bills that I needed to pay off. I thought that he would have been glad that I had GOALs and had a plan to take me to the next level of my life. Instead he told me that I was taking on too much and that everything seemed so unattainable. He said that having all those bills in plain view was flat out depressing and I should take them down before other people saw them. I knew that I couldn't keep running from my debt and the only way to fix the problem was to face it. So I didn't listen to him because I knew that by constantly seeing the problem I would eventually fix it.

At one point, the whole wall on the left side of my room had bills tacked all over it and it seemed like it would take me a lifetime to pay them off, but I just focused on one at a time. Every time I paid one off and removed it from the wall, I felt like a weight was lifted off my shoulders. That was years ago, eventually, there were no more bills left. Since then I relocated to a bigger city that had more opportunities; I got my college degree (which was a GOAL on my *Wish List*), and I am debt free. I got every single thing on that list and made another list with even bigger GOALs. As for him, he's still at the same place in his life. Today I'm glad that I didn't tear the list down and just give up like he suggested. *You don't have to explain your list to anyone because no matter how you try to break it down, some people will never get it…and that's okay, as long as you don't allow them to discourage you and let you feel like your GOALs aren't attainable. If people want you to lose your list, lose them instead!*

Lesson: #11. **Your list will be your first step to achieving a better life. Put it up on your wall above your bed, on your bathroom mirror or on your fridge.**

If you are a visual person, you can tear out pictures from magazines and put them up all over your home. You may have a GOAL of growing your hair, getting a nice car, getting your dream home, or losing weight. Find inspirational pictures and keep them in plain view for motivation. *Believe it and you'll achieve it.*

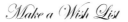

MY WISH LIST

Make sure your potential sponsors are listed under a code name or alias only (in case your list falls in the wrong hands).

Items I Want (short-term)   **Potential Sponsors**

_____   _____

_____   _____

_____   _____

_____   _____

_____   _____

_____   _____

_____   _____

_____   _____

_____   _____

_____   _____

_____   _____

_____   _____

A Gold Digger's Guide

Items I Want (long-term)   ## Potential Sponsors

_____   _____

_____   _____

_____   _____

_____   _____

_____   _____

_____   _____

_____   _____

_____   _____

_____   _____

_____   _____

_____   _____

_____   _____

Make a Wish List

Places I Want To Go

_____

_____

_____

_____

_____

_____

_____

_____

_____

_____

_____

_____

Potential Sponsors

_____

_____

_____

_____

_____

_____

_____

_____

_____

_____

_____

_____

(One of the places on my *Wish List* is Paris, France. Keep reading to see if I ever make it there)

Short-term GOALs I need to accomplish:

_____
_____
_____
_____
_____
_____
_____
_____
_____
_____
_____

Long-term GOALs I need to accomplish:

_____
_____
_____
_____
_____
_____
_____
_____
_____

Make sure you list a date beside each GOAL that you set so that you have deadlines and timelines to work within.

Make a Wish List

Steps I need to take in order to meet those GOALs:

_____
_____
_____
_____
_____
_____
_____
_____
_____
_____
_____
_____

Things that I need to work on:
(e.g., punctuality, personality or patience)

_____
_____
_____
_____
_____
_____
_____
_____
_____
_____
_____
_____

Influential people I want to meet:

_____
_____
_____
_____
_____
_____
_____
_____
_____
_____
_____

Steps that I need to take in order to meet them:

_____
_____
_____
_____
_____
_____
_____
_____
_____
_____
_____
_____

Make a Wish List

Debt I need to pay off   **Amount Owed**

_____ $_____

_____ $_____

_____ $_____

_____ $_____

_____ $_____

_____ $_____

_____ $_____

_____ $_____

_____ $_____

Notes:

_____

_____

_____

_____

_____

_____

_____

_____

_____

THE NEXT CHAPTER COVERS:

Picture Life as a Stadium

"Identifying" Technique

"Dumb Down" Technique

Looking in the Right Places

Actions Speak Louder Than Words

Low Profilers

Chapter 3

DO YOUR RESEARCH

...If You Fail to Plan, You Plan to Fail.

**The major component in GOAL setting is planning
thoroughly and following through.**

<u>Do Your Research</u>

I n life there are **spectators** and there are **players.** I believe that what separates me from most women is that I realize that there are more than just two playing fields. Most women were never schooled in looking beyond those two. Make it a point to be surrounded by intelligent people, quick thinkers and people who have a business mentality. I was fortunate enough to have met a few fellows who really taught me the game, took me under their wings, and pushed me to think outside of the box. One even went as far as giving me "homework" (a printout of the bio of the next person he was going to introduce me to). Sometimes I had only about five minutes before the introduction to learn about that person's personal life, education, work history, hobbies and colleagues. If you never had that type of influence, don't worry because what you need to know is within these pages.

Most women think that the **players** are at the top of the pyramid but they aren't; they are merely appetizers at the bottom of the food chain. Once you grasp that concept, then you start seeing the bigger picture. When I say "**players**" I'm not talking about guys who mistreat women, nor am I referring to professional athletes. It may be any guy that you may think has a lot going for himself; he may drive a nice car, live in a fancy home, have a college degree or work for a Fortune 500 Company and earn a five-figure income. To most women he has it going on, but I'm not swayed that easily. He may look shiny on the outside but chances are his car or house isn't paid off. **Translation:** *Most of his paycheck goes to paying bills which leaves fewer funds for him to splurge on you.* So yes, he may have nice things but don't ignore the fact that he probably has very high mortgage and car payments and, if his income stopped suddenly, he'd be no better off than you. What would happen if he was injured and couldn't work anymore? Exactly! You shouldn't be interested in a rich man; you should seek out the wealthy. There is a difference. Rich can disappear with one visit from the IRS, but wealth is backed by old and long money that is generations strong. I am more interested in the person that endorses the player's paycheck and owns that Fortune 500 Company and you should be too.

Lesson: #12. _If you come across a wealthy person, ask them if you can sit in on their next business meeting._ _If that's not possible then ask them to recommend a book for you to read or share with you an important lesson in life that they wished they'd learned sooner._

PICTURE LIFE AS A STADIUM

Whether you'd like to admit it or not, a major *game* is being played. By not acknowledging it, you are preparing to lose. In a metamorphic sense, life is a stadium. In life there are four sections: the stands, the field, the sidelines and the skybox. The **Spectators** watch the game from the stands; they purchase sports apparel and memorabilia, aspiring to be like their favorite sports stars. The **Players** are the stars on the field, very much playing the *game* and admired by many. The **Players** look up to the **Coaches** who give them strategies from the sideline and advice on how to play and win the game (the **Coaches** are ok, but you really shouldn't be content until you get the **Owner**). The **Owners** of the teams sit in the skybox and observe everything that goes on. They seem untouchable. They don't deal with the **Players** directly; in fact, their *game plan* is relayed through the coaches. The **owners** are right up my alley; they make the real money and are the only ones not being pimped. So know your role and be aware of the sections.

The **Spectators**: In a social setting the **Spectator** will probably be hanging near the ladies room, just waiting to pounce on women who exit. B*y the way, that's an annoying and desperate move.* Some **Spectators** kick it up a notch and hang out by the bar, waiting for a woman to walk up and buy her own drink so he can start a conversation with her. These are the ones in the "nose bleed" section; they'll never be in VIP. They are the ones usually decked out in knock offs and fake jewelry trying to imitate the **Player's** swag.

The **Players:** We all know who they are: the rappers, singers, comedians, actors and athletes. In a social atmosphere you'll find the **Players** in the VIP section. They usually never leave that area unless they're going to the restroom. So if you're feeling desperate, and the chances of making it in VIP are slim you can "accidentally" bump into a Player in the hallway to the bathroom (hallway of desperation).

Lesson: #13. ***Form partnerships with Coaches.*** ***Allow them to be your mentors.***

The **Coaches** usually work behind the scenes. They come in different forms and a variety of career fields. To most people they may be directors, producers, promoters, even chauffeurs and concierges…but I consider them mentors.

The **Players** know who they are because they deal with them directly every day, but the **Coaches** are often overlooked by everyone else. They don't necessarily make more money than the **Players**, but if you form a strong relationship with the **Coaches** they can take you a very long way. **Players** are replaceable, they come and go like the seasons. In fact, their average career span is eight years and by the end of their careers most of them are right back where they started financially. The **Coaches'** career span is usually much longer. They can show you the *play-book* and tell you *the plays* (who will be where and when, where you should be and what's coming up next). For example, if you have a friend that is an NBA commentator, your friendship could work out perfectly because he's not limited to just one team. He knows the whereabouts of all the teams at all times.

Lesson: #14. ***When you learn how to spot the Owners, you'll start spotting them for the rest of your life.***

The **Owners** run the show. Most of them are low-key and don't dress to impress because they've already reached a comfortable place in their lives and they know who they are. They know that they don't have to prove anything to anyone. A wealthy friend of mine once told me that he doesn't dress flashy because if no one suspects that he has money, no one will ask him for any. Another friend of mine owns a couple of record labels, but when women ask him what he does for a living, he says that he drives trucks. So ask around and verify the facts, but never make your inquisitiveness obvious to the **Owner** himself. The only way you'll find out who the **Owners** are is by tuning in to their actions and by doing your research in the short amount of time that you may have. Some things to tune into is how they walk, how they shake your hand, and mostly how they're treated by others- they all exude power and confidence. Most of the time it's the people around them that are the dead giveaways. For example: I remember one time I was on the set of a TV show, and I didn't know who the director was, but as soon as he stepped in the room everyone got silent. That was a very obvious indication that he held a power position. If you suspect that someone holds a power position but you aren't quite sure then just watch the actions of the people around him. If they are showing signs of nervousness, e.g., they're a bit stiff, they won't make eye contact with him, they're twiddling their fingers, playing in their hair or they've lowered their voice to a whisper, then your hunch is probably correct. The **Owners** supervise the directors, promoters, and other **Coaches** (middlemen). The **Owners** make the real decisions and make the real money.

"IDENTIFYING" TECHNIQUE

Lesson: #15. Do the Switch-a-Roo. Find out what he is accustomed to and do the total opposite.

You have to handle different types of guys accordingly. If he is *a guy that rarely gets any attention* then smile at him or throw a few compliments his way. If you are feeling really generous you can give him one of those church hugs with a pat on the back and a huge gap between you both. Who knows what may happen if you stroke his head...the one on his shoulders.

Then there is the type of *guy who is accustomed to getting his way* from women with hardly any effort, (usually because he's handsome, dresses nice, has a powerful position, drives a nice car, or he or his daddy has money). Some guys who have money go way overboard to make sure women take notice. By this I mean that they'll probably walk up to the cash register and take out a wad of cash even though their purchase may amount to a mere $10. Simultaneously they'll glance at you out of the corner of their eyes to see if you are watching, (just pathetic). They have many ways in which they show just how much they crave attention. They make their engines roar loudly when they drive by you. *They have no clue how much that turns a woman off.* For these guys that behave like temper-tantrum-throwing toddlers, handle them simply by ignoring them. Talk on your cell phone, freshen up your make-up, excuse yourself and go to the restroom, anything, other than giving them satisfaction by feeding into their antics.

"DUMB DOWN" TECHNIQUE

Lesson: #16.   *Never let a guy know all you know.*

The dumb down technique usually works on guys who love to be in control all of the time. While it's true that no one wants a dumb woman long-term, it's a fact that most males are intimidated by a female that's smarter than them. So disguising your intellect won't be such a bad idea at times because after all you aren't in this for the long haul. If a guy underestimates your intelligence and doesn't know your thoughts, then he won't know what you are capable of. He'll expect the least from you and you'll be able to catch him off-guard. Be very selective with this technique; you'll have to be on your guard because he may think that he'll be able to get away with some slick moves.

...Google is your best friend

__Lesson: #17.__ In your research efforts Google and Wikipedia.com are your friends. Everything on the internet may not be 100% true but assume that everything you read has some truth to it. It's a good research tool for information on people and events.

A few years ago my commentator friend introduced me to an NBA player. He was cute. He was medium brown and about five feet eleven inches tall; he had braids and light brown eyes. He and I talked over a bottle of Dom Perignon and he seemed like a cool person...until I Googled him on my Blackberry. I found an article which stated that he was accused of doing some dehumanizing acts to his ex-wife. It wasn't my job to cast a guilty or innocent verdict, but it was my intention to get the hell out of there as fast as I could...and I did.

__Lesson: #18.__ If you do what you have always done, then you'll get what you always got.

LOOKING IN THE RIGHT PLACES

Your way may not have worked for you in the past, but as long as you recognize it and you are willing to learn new techniques then things are going to get better for you from here on out. You want to find guys that can help you get ahead right? Well stop wishing and start planning, because chances are you're not just going to bump into them on the streets. You have to constantly step outside of your box. If you get comfortable doing something that previously made you feel uncomfortable then it means that you have grown and it's time to tackle new grounds. Wealthy people are among you, you just have to start participating in the same activities and festivities as they do. Visit art museums, science centers, fund-raising events, and auctions.

...Learn to narrow down the search

-If a *doctor* is your target, then get an entry-level job at a hospital.

-If it's a *lawyer* that you are after, then get an internship at a law firm, intern for a judge, or even apply to be a clerk at a courthouse.

- If you are looking for a *realtor*, or someone in the investment field then start going to real estate retreats and financial seminars and join investment clubs.

- If you are looking for a *CEO*, you could scout around the convention center in your area. If you need a specific reason to get into the building, call and say you're interested in booking a conference room, but you'd like to see the place first. By requesting a tour of the place you can get close to your target.

- If you are looking for an *athlete*, try to find out which hotels they usually stay in when they have games in your city. The athletes usually check in under code names so if you apply for a job as a front-desk clerk, you'll have the inside scoop.

- If you are looking for an *entertainer*, popping up at his concert is not going to do the trick. You have to deal with that challenge from the inside. Apply to be an intern at a record label or a recording studio.

- If you are looking for a guy that is a bit loose with his money then target *gamblers.* NASCAR, casinos, dog tracks, and horseracing tracks are great spots to find them.

- If you are looking for someone a bit *mature*, chances are slim that you'll find him in a night club. Scout out classy lounges, open mic events, piano bars, cigar lounges, wine tasting events, tennis matches, comedy shows, and jazz bars. Make yourself easily approachable, so leave your girlfriends home for this task.

- If you are looking for a *retiree* who has the flexibility to travel without worrying about vacation time (in other words, one who has a combination of time and money to spare), then get a job at a golf resort or country club. You should even start attending golf tournaments. Applying for a job at a yacht brokerage firm isn't a bad idea either.

- If you want someone who *drives a nice car* then apply for a job as a receptionist at a high-end car detailing shop. If you want to get more specific then get a job at a Benz, BMW, or Bentley dealership. I guarantee that anyone you meet there drives one of those cars...or will soon. ☺ *If you have a luxury car that needs serviced, (even though it may be an older model) don't hesitate to take it to the dealership.*

Basically, what I'm telling you is: instead of steering away from higher classed or expensive environments because you feel out of place, push your pride aside and go for it! Get right up there in the mix because that's the only way you're going to learn new things, make beneficial connections and meet influential people.

ACTIONS SPEAK LOUNDER THAN WORDS

Lesson: #19. *You have to study your target thoroughly in the limited amount of time that you have with him.*

If you observe a guy closely, you can quickly figure out a lot about him. When you just meet a guy he will put his best foot forward so you can't believe anything he tells you and you have to watch the signs. They all drop clues about their personality and true intentions. Some are more obvious than others; you just have to pay attention.

-If a guy buys you perfume, he may have bought the same scent that his ex usually wears, so he may not be over her, and you may be a rebound.

-If a guy never leaves his phone lying around and never wants you to meet him at his home, he may be hiding other women.

-If a guy gives you only his office number or work email then he may be married.

-If a guy wants to introduce you to his family, he probably wants a long-term relationship.

-If a guy brings up sex on the first date, he probably doesn't take you seriously or doesn't plan on keeping you around.

-If you just met a guy and he already planned out every detail of your date without even finding out your likes and dislikes, he's probably a womanizer and is just quickly going through his usual steps in order to get your goods.

-If he lives out of town and is willing to fly you to his city after just meeting you, it's probably a regular thing for him so don't feel special.

-If he is constantly giving you compliments and everything he says seems too perfect, rehearsed, or scripted, it probably is.

-When he asks you what you are looking for in a man, be careful how you answer because he is likely to become a chameleon to get what he wants.

LOW PROFILERS

Lesson: #20. *Never ask a guy what he does for a living unless he asks you first.*

You can coax it out of him but don't flat out ask, because you'll make it way too obvious that you are interested in his finances. Once he tells you what he does for a living ask him questions about his job like you actually care. For example, "You handle all that by yourself?" "How long did it take you to learn?" or "Can you teach me?" Tell him how smart he is, guys are suckers for compliments. *Massage his package and you'll have him only for that moment but massage his ego and you'll have him for a lifetime.*

The guys that spent the most money on me were **Low Profilers (LPs)**. They didn't dress flashy or flash their money in public. They rarely bragged or talked about what they did for a living. As a result they sometimes got overlooked by women, which left more money for me. They looked average because they hardly treated themselves to nice things, but if a woman looked at them twice they'd be glad to spoil her. You just have to constantly scan your atmosphere and look past the **Posers** that block the **LPs**. *(I talk more about **Posers** in Chapter Five).* You may get lucky and find an **LP** who doesn't expect sex, probably because he thinks that he can't get it. Having a meal with him or walking by his side is good enough. In many cases if you pay attention to the nerdy guy or the awkwardly dressed fellow in the back, you'll get more out of him than the popular guy because the popular one is already accustomed to the attention. Many times I've asked for ridiculous amounts of money from an **LP** after just meeting him to see if he would give it to me, and it worked. You can get it too, you just have to dress the part and make it seem like that is the type of treatment that you are accustomed to…and soon it will be.

THE NEXT CHAPTER COVERS:

Watering Holes

Some Useful information when you're on a date

Subjects to Get Educated In

Style

- Shoes
- Accessories
- Clothes that accentuate your body
- Hair
- Makeup

Simple Makeover Tips

Presence

Chapter 4

FAKE IT UNTIL YOU MAKE IT

...He'll Never Know the Difference.

Some people call it faking; others call it fitting in.

Fake It Until You Make It

The first time I read the title of this chapter to my friend James, he rapidly and excitedly responded that he would be able to taste the difference. He was a little bit disappointed when I replied that this chapter had nothing to do with faking an orgasm. When I say fake it until you make it, I mean: if you want to hang with and be accepted by the best of them then you have to fit in. You have to dress as they do, display similar mannerisms, know their lingo, and be able to keep up and participate in their conversations.

SUBJECTS TO GET EDUCATED IN

Wine - Go to a wine tasting event.
Cigars - Subscribe to Cigar Aficionado Magazine.
Tennis - Join your local tennis club.
Golf - Subscribe to Golf Magazine.
Fishing - Watch the World Fishing Network TV station.
Sailing - Subscribe to Sailing Magazine.
Travel - Watch the Travel Channel.
Foreign languages - Purchase Rosetta Stone software.
Art history - Visit art museums.
Philosophy - Search philosophy on Wikipedia.com.
Politics - Visit www.cnn/politics.com. & politics section of the news paper.
Real estate - Sign up for a Real Estate seminar.
Finance, the economy & stock market - Watch CNN and read the business section of the newspaper.
Some more cost-efficient ways to get educated on such matters is by taking classes at a community college,

attending lectures, joining book clubs or simply going to the library and reading. I made some educational videos about some of the previous subjects. Check out Baje's School of GOAL Digging on www.YouTube.com /HeyThereBuddyBJ. Your GOAL is to be interesting, so people are drawn to you and when the time calls for it you'll be able to hold a conversation of substance. *One website that I found beneficial to the development of vocabulary is WWW.Dictionary.com /wordoftheday.*

WATERING HOLES

f you have an option to relocate then choose
d that is better than your current one,
products of our environment.

There are a few cities in the US that are diverse and rich with people from different walks of life. I'm not just talking about athletes and entertainers. I'm talking about princes, sheiks, CEOs, and heirs. Visiting or residing in these places is essential to the GOAL Digging (GD) game. You can find great potential from all over the globe in these cities, with finances to tap into that seem endless. They usually don't live in those cities, but frequently visit them. Your chances of finding someone with the mentality and funds to spoil you soar in these areas. Most men who visit these places have no other intention but to splurge money on women, food, liquor, events, gambling, and entertainment in general. *Some of them spend large sums of money just to be seen at certain places.* So just by placing yourself in these environments you can accomplish your GOALs in less time, with less effort. Some huge *Watering Holes* include Dallas, Texas;

Manhattan, New York; South Beach, Florida; Las Vegas, Nevada and Hollywood, California. Watering holes don't always have to be major cities; they can be communities, venues or events. *I've listed a few, now it's up to you to Google them and find out more. If you know a watering hole, help me to help others by listing it on my site at AGoldDiggersGuide.com*

Communities: Greenwich Village, New York; the Hamptons; Star Island, Florida; Beverly Hills, California; Palm Springs, California; Palm Beach, Florida; Scottsdale, Arizona; Windermere, Florida.

Most states have a few cities or communities within it that the wealthy predominantly reside in.

Events: NBA Championship Games, NBA All Star Games, The Super Bowl, The Pro Bowl, World Series Baseball Games, World Heavyweight Boxing Championship, The Kentucky Derby, The Breeders Cup, The PGA Tour, The Masters Tournament, The US Open Tennis Tournament, The US Open Polo Tournament, The Grammy Awards, Emmy Awards, Republican conventions, Democratic conventions, The Inauguration.

Events may be your best option, because most are open to the public and in nearly all cases affordable tickets will be available for purchase. It doesn't matter what section of the building your ticket sentences you to, because once you're in the building it's your duty to find your way into the VIP section, sky box, etc.

Venues: Beverly Hills Hotel, Bel Air Hotel, Waldorf Astoria, Beverly Hilton, Beverly Wilshire, Peninsula, Fountainebleau, Park Ave Restaurant, Crustaceans Restaurant, Koi Restaurant, STK, Mr. Chows, Nobu, Tavern on the Green (NYC), Morton's The Steak House, Ruth's Chris. *Most of these particular venues happen to be hotels and restaurants in Los Angeles, California.*

One good thing about venues is that some have chains in several cities. For example: Smith & Wollensky is located in Miami, Chicago, Washington, Philadelphia, Las Vegas, Columbus, Houston and New York. The downside is that some venues are only open during certain seasons like Joe's Stone Crab and overall venues, are the least stable of the *Watering Holes* because in many cases they are at their best for only a year or two and then a new, hotter venue opens right next door.

For this reason especially, your networking game has to be immaculate. Once you are in a *Watering Hole*, make sure to find out who is in charge and make that connection: if you can't get to the head person in charge (the owner), his assistants will do. Once you make the connection ask questions and find out if there are other venues like that one or any other events coming up in the future. Make sure to keep the connection with those contacts, give them a call, or send them a text every so often (not just when you want information or something else from them).

SOME USEFUL INFORMATION WHEN YOU'RE ON A DATE

- Usually, the older the wine, the better tasting or more expensive it is.

- Red wine goes with red meat (such as steak) and white wine goes with white meat (such as turkey, chicken, pork and fish).

- If you're eating pasta, red wine goes with red sauce and white wine goes with white sauce.

- Red wines include: Merlot, Cabernet and Pinot Noir

- White wines include: Chardonnay and Sauvignon Blanc

- Blushes are like a mixture of both red and white wines (like White Zinfandel).

- Red wine is never chilled.

- Dessert wines are sweet and typically served with dessert, fruit, pastries, or alone.

-Dessert wines include: Moscato d'Asti and Port.

- Hang your purse on your chair or put it on your lap, but not the table.

- When there is a lot of silverware on the table, use the utensils on the outside first.

- Even if you have a straw lift the glass to your mouth. Don't slouch over to sip or slurp.

 - No matter how good the food is, leave a little bit on the plate.

 - When you are finished with your meal close the knife and fork by placing your knife in the middle of your fork prongs.

- When your date is over and if a guy opens the car door for you, when you get in the car reach over and open his door. Be prepared for him to ask you if you seen the movie "A Bronx Tale" because a woman in the movie did that same move.

I learned the basics of etiquette because I went to an all-girl boarding school for four years. I'd encourage you to take etiquette classes if you can.

…I've always had a taste for the finer things in life

I knew that I wanted a better life, so I was willing to take risks and do things that most people wouldn't, even if it meant relocating to unfamiliar cities. You have to make an effort to step outside of your comfort zone. At first you may feel out of place, but the more you take risks the easier it gets. Most of your friends may ask why you are moving, going to certain events or why you are hanging out with that type of crowd. Just know that you don't have to explain anything to anyone. Most people probably wouldn't understand or would try to talk you out of it because they are ruled by fear. They may even be a bit jealous that you are on to bigger and better things. I run a talent agency (GlitzAndGlamourModels.com) and I always tell my new talent that no one else knows that they are nervous unless they allow their jitters to get the best of them. I tell them that even if they feel out of place just play it off and never let people see them sweat. That simple piece of advice usually gets them through castings and auditions.

Lesson: #22. ***If you have champagne taste on a wine cooler budget don't worry, you just have to come up with a plan and gradually work toward it.***

It starts with your *mindset*, then your sense of *Style*, and last but definitely not least, your *Presence*. Once you combine all three fundamentals and shimmy your way to the right neighborhoods, events and settings then the type of guy that you are after will soon be after you.

Lesson: #23. ***Style is all about accentuating your best features and camouflaging your flaws.***

STYLE

In most cases you either have it or you don't. Luckily *Style* can be taught, imitated, or duplicated. Look through the latest fashion magazines (you don't have to buy them). Simply go into a bookstore and flip through some pages. You don't have to purchase the same exact outfits you see, just get a feel for the fabric and patterns and make a replica. If you are working with a tight budget go to Target and find similar items to arrange in the same fashion. You can also acquire ideas by going to the websites of some of the top designers like Chanel, Versace, Prada, Christian Dior, Louis Vuitton (LV), Dolce & Gabanna (D&G) or simply look at how the mannequins are dressed at an upscale mall or expensive store (like Nordstrom or Saks Fifth Avenue). *Keep in mind that knee-length skirts, scarves, and oversized sunglasses always add a touch of class.*

Lesson: #24. *You are allowed to wear inexpensive outfits, just make sure that they don't look cheap.*

If you see a nicely dressed woman, don't be shy to ask her where she purchased the items she is wearing *(even though her answer will probably that they were gifts, it doesn't hurt to try).* Women just hate giving away their little secrets, but when you see a woman that you consider stunning, pinpoint what it is about her that makes her stand out. If it's an item that can be bought, then add it to your *Wish List* for the next lucky fellow that you meet.

Lesson: #25. *A lot of males are turned on by sexy shoes on pretty feet.*

Shoes: Stilettos (thin, high heels) are always sexy. If you can't manage a four-inch heel then go lower. I suggest that you steer away from thick heels, because the wrong pair can ruin your whole outfit. However, make a mental note that wedge heels and pumps are making a comeback. Gold and silver are in because they'll go well with any color outfit. Besides skirts and dresses, pointy-toe shoes complement only flare jeans, not skinny jeans. That combo makes most women's feet look too big. Open-toed shoes can pretty much go with anything, just not flared or wide-leg jeans. If you don't have the prettiest toes you may want to steer away from showing them off.

__Lesson: #26.__ What you wear means nothing if you don't know how to wear it. Add some flavor and pizzazz, perfect your style, and make it your signature.

Accessories: Never underestimate jewelry (whether it is costume jewelry, or the real deal) because they really bring an outfit to life. A little bling goes a long way, but don't over-do it. You don't have to have earrings, a bracelet, and a necklace that bling. Keep it classy (KIC); just one or two pieces are fine. Every woman should own diamonds, *personally, they turn me on.* If you haven't been fortunate enough for a guy to treat you with a piece, then you should *invest* in one piece – it doesn't have to be expensive. If you are buying your first piece don't worry too much about the Cs (Carat, Cut, Color, or Clarity), just a little sparkle to open your appetite should be enough.

Clothes that accentuate your body: While it is true that every woman should have a little black "freak um" dress in her closet, do not make it a habit of wearing black in the night time because it is way too easy to blend in and be over looked. At an all white party (a party where the dress code is white), wear a red dress. I will guarantee you that everyone will notice you, and that is always the GOAL isn't it? As a backup have a white dress in your car in case you chicken out. Don't forget to cater to the crowd (CTC). If it's an urban function, then you know it's all about accentuating your bottom half. If it's another crowd then showing a little bit of cleavage usually gets the job done. Common sense is to know when to cover it all up, take off the "door knocker" earrings, put on some pearls, and pull your hair in a bun.

Lesson: #27. Get familiar with your body.

The same dress that looks amazing on your girlfriend may not look as hot on you. Fashion today is geared more towards the *80s era*, which is awesome for someone who has flaws to hide because most of the dresses and shirts have a very loose fit. If you have a very nice body, go against the fad and wear something form-fitting. If you are tall, thin, or have long legs you can wear skinny or flare jeans. If you are a woman on the thicker side, you may want to *invest* in some wide-leg jeans, because they are slimming. If you want to minimize a big booty, high-waist jeans will do the trick. If you want to give the illusion that you have a bigger booty then try low-cut jeans with pockets. Just make sure when you sit down you're not showing your crack. *If this is too much information for you to take in all at once, then feel free to Google a stylist in your area for a consultation.*

Hair: Layers and highlights are definitely a good look. You hardly see women wearing their hair dark or flat. More women are going for hair that has a bounce to it. The latest trendy "must have" that has taken over is the lace-front wig. Most of the wigs are made from human hair, start at $700 and come in a wide range of colors and styles to choose from. They look so natural; most women in Hollywood wear them now. They are expensive but well worth the cost, because they are durable, can be washed, and will last for years. You may be able to find some synthetic lace-fronts that start at $70 at your local hair store. If you are still wearing pinch plats, finger waves or multi-colored weaves then you're definitely going to need a major fashion make-over. If you lighten your hair it's also wise to lift the color of your eyebrows a shade or two. If you are apprehensive about doing so, there is an eyebrow lightener that you can get at Mac called brow set and it washes right off. *If one of your GOALs is to be "weave-free," then check out the Long Hair Care forum at* www.longhaircareforum.com. *It's the ultimate hair care and beauty resource.*

Lesson: #28. **Before make-up is applied, hygiene comes first! Fresh breath, manicures and pedicures are mandatory.**

Make-up: At first glance, when you look at a celebrity or a rich woman, the one thing that makes her stand out the most is her make-up. That's the major clue when distinguishing the VIPs from everyone else. *I mostly shop at Mac.* They have make-up for all skin types and tones and professionals onsite to show you how to apply everything flawlessly. They do makeovers right in the store for $40, which will come in handy when you have a big function to attend. The secret to having professional-looking make-up is all in the brushes, so throw away those little sponge tip applicators and *invest* in real brushes. You'll thank me later.

Find the best feature on your face and accentuate it, if it's your lips, wear a color or super shiny gloss that will make them pop, check out lip glass from Mac. Always use a lip liner before you apply your lipstick, it will appear so much neater. If it is your eyes that you like the most, then wear the color eye-shadows that complement your eyes the best. With eye-shadows it's all about blending. Most people wear three shades at a time, the first color highlights your eyebrows, the second color is usually a color close to your natural skin tone or a color that will complement the outfit that you are wearing, and the third color is usually a darker shade that goes on the crease of your eye lid. The Smoky eye is my favorite for a night time look.

If you don't have defined cheekbones you can cheat by contouring. Simply take a darker color blush or contouring powder and brush it on your cheek in an upward motion (not on the plump part of your cheeks when you smile but in the section right below your cheekbone).

Lesson: #29. *Looks capture attention, but personality captures the heart.*

Though looks may get you places, often times it will not keep you there. It pays to have talent, an unforgettable personality and character. Don't beat yourself up about your physical "imperfections" because most of the models you see in magazines are photo-shopped (altered using a computer program). So the flawless skin, the light-colored eyes, and the tiny little waistlines aren't always reality. *Don't strive to look like anyone else, just strive to be a better you.*

Lesson: #30. *Perfection is only perception. Learn to love you.*

A lot of women struggle with weight issues because they aren't motivated enough to stick to their workout regimens. They'll stop working out once they reach their desired weight so the weight comes back on or they'd rather eat a slice of chocolate cake than steamed vegetables. There is nothing wrong with that. Who decided the perfect global weight anyway? If you think you should work out or eat healthier for health reasons then by all means do so, but if you are happy with your weight then don't allow society to force you into a lifestyle of counting calories. Live to please you, it's your body, no one else should have a say about how much you weigh. Many women allow guys or a bathroom scale to determine their self esteem and influence their moods and thoughts; they shouldn't. No matter what shade or shape you may be, never forget that you are beautiful. If you aren't happy with your weight and made the decision to do something about it then surround yourself with people who are supportive, optimistic and who will keep you motivated. Until you start seeing results, don't be too harsh on yourself. I've had the pleasure of meeting many big women who are nothing short of Divas. Some would call it the "Mo'Nique Complex". Mo'Nique is a plus size woman that many are drawn to because she lights up every room that she steps into. Women like Mo'Nique would never allow anyone to talk down or even look down on them, because they know who they are and are proud of it. *Big or small, walk with confidence, hold your head up high and allow your inner Diva to shine through your smile.*

SIMPLE MAKEOVER TIPS

-If you have hair (peach fuzz) on your upper lip wax it (if you wax it, it will not grow back thicker but if you shave it, it will).

- If your teeth are a bit yellow use Crest White Strips; it works wonders and will save you $300 by not having to visit the dentist's office for professional whitening.

-If you're looking for a more inexpensive way to whiten your teeth, brush with pure baking soda every day.

-Never leave the house without lip-gloss, face powder for touch ups, and a brush for your hair. Don't forget perfume for a quick pick-me-up.

-Sunglasses always come in handy when you were up late the night before and aren't looking your best.

-If you have corns on your toes, use Dr. Scholl's liquid corn remover, in less than a week they'll be gone. (You can buy it get it at your local drug store).

-A pair of big earrings will make any outfit look snazzy at the last minute.

-When you can't decide on an outfit, go with a tank top and jeans because you can always accessorize by dressing it up with heels or dressing it down with sandals.

-If you get razor bumps easily, stop shaving and start waxing instead. Then start using a fading cream like Ambi or Symba for the old scars.

-For recent scars try Maderma – it's in a little white tube and costs $16 at your local drug store; it will make your scars less visible.

-If you get bags under your eyes, use two slices of cucumber or boil tea bags and put them on your eyes for a couple minutes. If that doesn't work, use Preparation H.

-For acne, try Pro Active. For a quick fix for big pimples apply some toothpaste for about thirty minutes, and then wash it off.

-If you want your breasts to seem fuller and can't afford or don't like the idea of plastic surgery then you can put silicone inserts in your bra (you can purchase them at Victoria Secret or Target stores).

-If you have naturally dark lips, use a neutral color lipstick, it will even out the tone.

-If you have a bad scar, a burn or a birthmark that you want to hide, try Dermablend. It gives the best coverage for that type of problem. You can purchase it at Dillard's or any other department store.

-If you want longer nails, but want to avoid the damage of acrylic, try Deceptions Press on Nails. You can find them in the beauty supply section at your local drugstore.

PRESENCE

When you walk in a room, walk in with confidence; always be aware of your poise and posture. Whatever room you walk into is your house. Own it! Walk in alone because this is your moment to shine and you don't need anyone stealing your thunder. If you drove with friends, right before you walk in, take out your cell phone and say you have to make a quick call. Tell them that they should just go in and you'll meet them inside in a moment.

Lesson: #31. **_Don't hold a conversation with a guy if he doesn't offer you a drink, it's about the principle._** **_(If you've had enough, he should at least give you the option to say no)._**

When you walk into a venue, scan the main room and the VIP section quickly. Going straight to the restroom gives you the perfect opportunity, because in most establishments it's all the way in the back (*plus when you are walking with a destination in mind you won't seem like you're intentionally scanning the room*). This gives you an idea of what section of the building you'll choose to be at for most of the night, because it's tacky to float around and make it obvious that you are *scouting*. On the walk to the restroom hopefully you spotted your *Money Man* (M&M) *and if you did, then follow steps 1-5 on the next page.* If not, then on your return from the restroom, go straight to the bar and order a beverage, *as if you actually intend to pay for it yourself.* By beverage I do mean a glass of sparkling water, garnished with a slice of lime (which is usually free). *You can always switch it out for the drink that you really want later on when a man comes up to you.* In the meantime it just looks better to guys watching, knowing that a woman can hold her own if she chooses to.

A guy will be more drawn to a woman who looks capable of buying her own drink for one of two reasons:

> **1.** He's cheap and now he can use the line, "I was going to offer you a drink but you already have one."

Or

2. He's attracted to independent women.

For your sake hopefully you buying your own "drink" will attract the latter of the two.

If you need more time while you are at the bar then take out your cell phone and text or call someone…anyone. If you get their voicemail feel free to leave a message. If you *still* need more time then give the bartender your debit card and tell him that you want to start a tab (all this means is that you won't get charged per drink, instead he'll just close out the transaction at the end of the night). By not having to pay for your drink just then, it gives you more time for someone to come up to you and offer to buy you a drink.

If you spot your **M&M,** make sure you stay within his sight. This is where your presence or essence comes into play because if you are on point he'll come to you.

1. Don't make it too obvious that he has your attention.

2. Make sure that you stay within his peripheral vision so he doesn't get sidetracked – *we all know how short men's attention spans are.*

3. Don't entertain conversation with any other guys that come up to you because when you seem like a challenge, oddly guys will find you even more attractive.

4. When you turn down the other guys, don't seem too harsh because if your **M&M** is watching you, you still want him to think that he has a chance. Once you make eye contact with him give him a flirtatious smile, at this point he'll probably signal you to come over to him.

5. When he does signal for you to come over, don't go. Instead tell him to come to you, let him work for you to show him that you're not a groupie. If he does...you got him! If you have a strong presence or make a good impression then he should be eager to approach you.

Note: if you ask him what he's drinking and he doesn't offer to buy you something right then, Honey, throw that one back in and keep fishing because if he's a gentleman then that's his cue to offer. After reading this book you should have enough confidence and knowledge to lead the conversation and bend it in the direction that you want it to go in.

If your **M&M** doesn't come to you it's not a big deal, keep it moving (KIM). You want a guy that doesn't have a problem taking directions or following instructions. It doesn't matter how much money he has, if he isn't willing to work on your terms or give you what you want then he is useless.

Note: You must be fully prepared to pay for anything that you order in the event that a guy doesn't come up to you in time to take care of your bill. This is why I stress self-sufficiency and making your *own* money, just in case things don't go according to plan. *Sometimes it takes money to make money.* Sometimes even if you are going on a date and he'll pay for dinner, you may have to pay for parking, valet, or tip the doorman if your date is already seated inside.

Lesson: #32. *Staying at an event until the lights come on or until the DJ starts playing slow jams brings your stocks down. You have to seem as if you have somewhere else to be.*

When it's time to leave, never stay until the end of the event unless there is more potential in a more exclusive room that you just haven't had a chance to get to yet. Which brings me to my next point: always seem like you are in high demand. When a guy asks if you are available tomorrow or the following day, don't respond too quickly or with too much enthusiasm. Tell him that you'll have to check your schedule. If he asks you if he can meet up with you this weekend or next week, tell him that you can't make plans that far in advance, because something else (like making money) may come up. Tell him you'll call him the day of or the night before if you're available. Keep him in suspense. Remember that your time is the most important thing on earth. It's the one thing that can't be bought and when it's gone you can't get it back so make sure that the person that you choose to spend it with is worth it. There were many nights that I went out and didn't get one phone number because I know what I want, and I will not settle. When I step into an establishment I have the no nonsense look on my face; I stay towards the back and away from the crowd, because I don't want to be approached by the desperate guys that just circle the club and grab the first woman that they see standing alone. If a guy that I'm not interested in finally works up the nerve to walk up to me, I keep the conversation very short or simply treat him like he's a telemarketer and give him the "I'm not interested" reply.

One of the most unusual experiences I had was at the official after-party for the BET Awards at the Roosevelt Hotel.

Guys were coming at me all night back to back. They'd see other guys talking to me and as soon as one walked off another one would take his place. I remember two guys walked up to me at the same time and one said to the other, that it was okay, he'd wait his turn and he actually did. He waited right there until I dismissed the other guy and then he went into his speech. *That night was hilarious.* I shooed most of them away but there was one that I decided to hold a conversation with that night. He happened to be a comedian by profession. At first I kept my answers short until finally he said that he was just going to walk away because he ran out of things to say. I couldn't help but laugh, something about him was cute and vulnerable, plus he looked like a young Chris Tucker so I told him to stay a little longer.

THE NEXT CHAPTER COVERS:

How to Memorize His Phone Number

Coyote Shots and Lemon Drops

Posers and Preachers

Paper or Plastic

SECTION: II

Play the Game to Win

Chapter 5

STRATEGIZE AND EXECUTE

...Keep Your Eyes On The Prize.

When things aren't going according to plan and you feel like giving up, that's when you need to try even harder; that's the point when quitters subside and winners surface.

Strategize and Execute

Lesson: #33. **Celebrities are most sought after when very little is known about their personal lives. Follow their example and keep your personal life to yourself. Your target doesn't need to know about your brother the jail bird or your baby father drama.**

D on't make it a habit of giving out your phone number. The less people know about you, the more intriguing you become. Be discreet. Besides, it just looks tacky if you give it out to more than one person at the same venue. Just take his business card. If he doesn't have one or gives you the excuse that he just gave away his last one, then this is your chance to be different…by memorizing it. He'll be mesmerized.

Lesson: #34. **Never fiddle with your cell phone while a guy is talking to you and if he takes his phone out of his pocket, then immediately tell him to put it away. If either of you have your phone in hand while you're speaking to each other, it seems as if you're exchanging contact info and that defeats the purpose of being discreet.**

HOW TO MEMORIZE HIS PHONE NUMBER

Some would say I have a photographic memory because once I repeat digits, I'm able to picture them in my mind and I can remember them. If you don't have a very good memory, then try the following method. Within the first five minutes of your conversation with a guy, he'll probably tell you where he is from. Pay attention to that because more than likely his area code will correspond with his hometown. For example, if he's from Atlanta, his area code will probably be 404 or 678. *If you know the prefix for the phone numbers for most of the major cities then you are already a step ahead.* Once he tells you his area code then associate it with something or someone. For example, you may have a cousin named Jane that lives in that same city. Secondly, break down the next three digits (like 534). It may be the same three digits in your brother Tim's phone number. Then study the last four digits (if you pay close attention you'll find a way to tie it to something). It may be your birth year (like 1985) or the building number for a street that you use to live on (like 2310 Pine Street). Having an image of "Jane, Tim and Pine Street" may help you to memorize your target's phone number. By repeating "Jane and Tim went to Pine Street" or simply singing the numbers (to yourself of course) will increase your chances of remembering it until you have a chance to go to the restroom and write it down.

Lesson: #35. *Your actions should never be predictable.*

You will probably be the first woman to use this technique on him so don't be surprised if he looks a bit apprehensive or if he says that he doesn't think that you're going to call him. That reaction is actually welcomed because it's evidence that you are in control (*you now have the golden touch*). Tell him that you wouldn't waste your time standing there if you weren't going to call. Once he tells you his number, simply walk away. No "good bye," no "see you later," nothing. You don't owe him an explanation. It will keep him on his toes and will be a nice surprise when he actually does receive your highly anticipated phone-call. Trust me, he'll be impressed.

Lesson: #36. *Whichever method you use, the key to remembering his phone number is to say it repeatedly but more importantly you have to write it down within the following three minutes.*

Most guys will keep talking to you after they give you their phone number and that will surely make you forget it; that's exactly why I say you should immediately walk away. If he asks you if you'll remember his number, tell him:

"Not if you don't walk away now."

If he's *still* trying to talk to you then tell him that he just made you forget it and then you walk away. The last thing you want is a guy who can't follow instructions. If he's giving you that much trouble on day one, it's only going to get worse.

Lesson: #37. *Who bends first loses. If you lose, don't lose the lesson!*

I have encountered two guys who were very strong-minded. One was a smooth-talking, muscular brother from the hit reality show "I love New York" (I met him while I was working at Jamie Foxx's 40th birthday party in Miami). When he asked me for my phone number I told him that I don't give it out and he simply said,

"Well neither do I."

He extended his hand for me to shake, and said:

"It was nice to meet you."

I shook his hand and then he just walked off. Later that night I bumped into him again and this time around he gave me his number, but time proved that he was one of the toughest guys to get through mentally.

The second strong-minded guy was slim, brown-skinned, about 6 feet 3 inches tall, with a bald head. From his physique I could tell that he played basketball. He walked away from me because he wanted to exchange numbers and that is against my policy, so I told him that I would only take his. He being able to just walk away from me showed me that he wasn't an ordinary fellow. Five minutes later I went to the bouncer and asked him to give me the 411 on that guy and then I told the bouncer to bring him to me, which he did. When he came over to me he asked, "Oh, now you want to talk to me?" I told him that the only reason I was giving him my card was because he was strong enough not to give in to my request. I gave him my card and then I walked away. He never called; he happened to be an NBA player that was a member of the Celtics (they won the championship that very week).

If a guy walks away from you and it is really someone that you are interested in, your immediate reaction will be to go after him or compromise and give him your number. Resist the urge. I went against my instincts twice and it didn't work out in my favor. With that being said, my tactics don't always work, which isn't necessarily a bad thing because from that NBA player's behavior that night I know that I would have had problems molding him in the future. Guys of this stature see hundreds of women in a week. They've seen and heard all types of "game"; you'll have to handle them differently. Most importantly, you have to ask yourself if you are up for the challenge. Personally, I know that I am not. I have much more on my mind then trying to figure out, chase, or change a man. I would rather get the ones that I know will give me what I want without putting up a fight or stressing me out. Wouldn't you? If you want a guy in the limelight, ask yourself if you'll be able to constantly compete for his attention.

While most women go after guys who throw fake bills in the air for the camera or the characters that rent houses, rims, cars and even girls for their videos, I've come to appreciate a different style of fellow (*like the **Owner** I m ʰʲoned in Chapter Three*). In defense of females in the ⸝   ᵉnt field and contrary to popular beliefs: most consider videos just a gig and they go straʲ Sure there are some sad cases who have beyond the call of duty for some extra canʳ aren't the majority.

I find it amusing how some gravitate to the biᵍ chains like little ferrets. *Ooh look at the shiny coloᵣᵥ* they are pulled by a magnetic force. I hate to steal youᵣ thunder, but not all those blinged out pieces are real. I've heard cases of some artists that have the real deal and they take it to the pawn shop on a regular basis, *as I mentioned previously, but that's beside the point.* If that is who does it for you then go for it, but keep in mind that it's all about strategy. I've observed that the woman who is right in front of the *stars* striving for their attention is usually the one who gets overlooked. It's usually the woman in the back, sitting by herself, checking her text messages and paying them absolutely no attention that they find intriguing. *You should try it sometime.* Whenever you go to events make sure to place yourself in an area where you can see the entrance because you have to know who is in the building at all times.

Lesson: #38. Pay extra attention to the alleyways and the backdoors, because those are the entrances that most big money guys use to get in and out of the building.

Make it a habit to introduce yourself to the DJ and don't be afraid to ask him or the security guards, "who is in here?" and they'll know exactly what you mean. In fact, ask the doorman the same question before you enter the building to evaluate if it is even worth going inside.

Lesson: #39. It's all about location. If you have all the right moves, but you are in the wrong place then it is worse than not having any moves at all.

No matter where you may relocate to, always try to stay near the heart of the city. It may be a little more expensive, but in most cases its worth because the real money never stays in the building too long. They make cameos - they pop in, pop a few bottles, and then they're gone like the wind. It's beneficial for me to be only a few blocks away from the hot spots because when my inside contact sends me a text and says come through, I'm there within the hour because I know its money time. My inside contact doesn't even have to tell me exactly who is in the building, because it's already established between us who I will or will not roll out of bed for. I jump in the shower, slip on a dress, tease my weave, and I'm out.

Just because someone is famous doesn't mean that he has a lot of money...but that's another story. Most women go after the celebrities. I wouldn't recommend that because everyone else is also after them. You'll probably meet them in a social setting and may hang out with them the next day, but for most women that's about it. More times than not, celebrities with very little time and a lot of money are not going to take you seriously if they met you in that kind of atmosphere. Therefore, you have to decide what it is that you want to get out of the situation. If you just want to hang out with them, be seen and travel on the tour bus from city to city (which is a huge groupie move and not my style) then this is how you do it. Get to know his brother, friend or even better, his bouncer. The celebrity himself is looking for new meat in each city that he visits. He's not trying to bring the girl he met last night to another city; she's old news- *you don't bring sand to the beach right?* By establishing a friendship with his colleagues you'll manage to stay in the circle longer. They'll be glad for the unexpected attention because so many of them get lost in the shadows.

Hanging around them is one thing, but how they treat you is another thing. If you act like a groupie you'll get treated accordingly. You don't have to be uptight and you don't have to be in the "no zone" the whole time. It is okay to enjoy yourself and if someone ever crosses the line just say no. *No is a very powerful word.* In the midst of all this, remember that you teach guys how to treat you by setting boundaries and holding them accountable for their actions. I worked on set with over thirty R&B and rap artists and have never been disrespected. I don't give out the type of energy that indicates that insolence is acceptable...because it never is.

Lesson: #40. ***Make your target feel comfortable. You'll find that he will do more for you when he isn't under pressure.***

Surprisingly, often guys tell me that they feel like they've known me for a long time, and here is the reason. I am comfortable in my own skin and others recognize that trait quickly because it shows in my mannerisms. If I am on a guy's turf (which isn't often), instead of asking him for something to drink, I'll tell him WHEN I'm going in his fridge. I don't wait for him to tell me that I can have a seat or get comfortable, within a few minutes I'm kicking off my shoes, propping my feet on his couch and telling him to bring me a light snack. If there are dishes in the sink I may wash a few if I'm in a good mood. If my cell phone rings, I may ask him to tell me who is calling or even answer it. All these gestures throw his guards off. If you are comfortable and at ease, he will be to, and chances are you'll end up getting a better response out of him.

...Role play

You have to pick a role that you want to play and stick with it. I usually assume the sister role (or concierge if you want to get technical). I assume this role only for the guys that I actually find it beneficial to hang out with in the long run. I'll arrange for a driver to chauffeur them around town, I'll show them the hotspots, call the venue ahead of time and reserve the table, tell them what areas and people to stay away from and hire armed body guards if needed. I also don't interfere if they decide to talk to women that are more their speed.

It's unbelievable what some women are willing to do for next to nothing because too many women are star-struck. As soon as they spot a celebrity, their eyes widen and their jaws drop. Celebrities are only people like you and me. Some women succumb to alcohol and lose their inhibitions and composure. After they consume the free alcohol that is offered in large quantities their behaviors change drastically. Before they know it they're feeling incredibly sexy and doing things that they previously swore that they'd never do. Gradually, persistent guys will get the women's guards down as the panties follow. Maybe you've heard at least one story of an intoxicated woman waking up the next morning trying to figure out what she did and didn't do the night before.

He, on the other hand will probably already be in another city. If the woman did get a phone number from him, it was probably the "Ho line" or the "Bat phone" which is his second phone that his main girl knows nothing about. Many times it's just a voicemail that's checked once monthly. *Ladies, you have to be smarter…this is where Coyote Shots and Lemon Drops come into play.*

<u>COYOTE SHOTS and LEMON DROPS</u>

Guys love to do shots with women. Why is that? They know that they weigh considerably more than us, and they can consume much more alcohol than we can before they experience any effects? It would be detrimental to the GD game for me to tell you to turn down all drinks that are offered to you, but I will say this...

Lesson: #41. Don't stay in the "No Zone" the whole time.

Ever wondered why a lot of men like blondes? Contrary to most beliefs all blondes aren't dumb, (hair color has nothing to do with intelligence). However, for some reason over the years blondes have been portrayed as "happy go lucky," easygoing and extremely open-minded. Kind of how most people are after a few cocktails right? When you tell most men that you do not drink alcohol and you turn down all drinks offered, then immediately red flags go up in their heads. They may even view you as a threat because they know that you are composed and well aware of your surroundings. In other words: they know that your guards are up and its harder or even impossible for them to lure you into bed. If their main priority is to get you into bed and they think that there is absolutely no chance of doing so, then they may start holding back. So imagine how at ease they would be if they thought you were inebriated but you actually weren't. You'd get to see their true intentions in half the time; *which brings me to a clever trick I learned from a movie that came in handy. The movie was called Coyote Ugly and it featured Tyra Banks.* If you're challenged to do a shot, order an energy drink also, (you'll have to drink some of the energy drink first in order to make room in the can). Every time you put the liquor in your mouth *act* like you are chasing it with the energy drink– but you're going to coyly spit the shot in the energy can. I call it a *Coyote Shot.* If you don't think that you can do it smoothly then stick to a code drink, e.g., *Lemon Drop.* Tell the bartender ahead of time that if you order a *Lemon Drop* then that's your code drink for the night, so he shouldn't put any alcohol in it. If you find a cool bartender you both can split the money from all those fake drinks that guys bought for you at the end of the night.

I remember one time a guy made a bet with me that I couldn't do more shots of Patron than him. So while we were arguing back and forth I signaled a code to one of my girls to put water in my shot glasses and the real deal in his. Every time I took a fake shot I made an ugly face and acted like I was going to throw up, it was hilarious. *How foolish would I be going shot for shot with a grown man?* After he got sloppy drunk I told him what I did.

Lesson: #42. Never accept a drink from a guy if you didn't see him open the bottle or if you didn't see the bartender pour it. Walk with him to the bar if you have to and never ever leave your drink unattended.

Don't trust anyone to watch your drink. It's not a matter of will they slip something in your drink, but it's almost guaranteed that they will not watch it as closely as you would. One thing to be aware of is guys with long fingernails. I've heard cases where they'd keep powdered drugs under their fingernails and secretly release it into unsuspecting women's drinks. A couple of years ago, a girlfriend of mine had two drinks at a party and woke up the next morning in a room with two guys she didn't know and couldn't even remember how she got there. I'm sure you can only imagine what happened. My guess is that someone slipped a date-rape drug in her drink.

<u>Lesson: #43.</u> *Avoid Drugs…especially illegal ones.*

…Go Fish

<u>Lesson: #44.</u> *Allow the sardines to keep you looking good until the big fish comes along.*

Over your lifetime you'll be approached by guys from all walks of life, so understand that most of them can contribute to your cause…even if it's a little. Analyze each one thoroughly. If you can't get cash from them, you may be able to extract some sort of service. Don't only set your eyes on the big fish because the sardines can come in handy in the meantime. Don't get discouraged because even though the big ones don't come as often, if you play your cards right, the wait will be well worth it. All your life you are going to have to spend money on small things, and trust me, they do add up. So until the big fish bites your bait, *Tom* can wash your car, *Dick* can cut your grass, and *Harry* can hook you up with his buddy pass.

…Birds of a Feather

Three girlfriends (Lacy, Lexima, Holly) and I took a road trip to New Orleans for All Star Weekend. It took us twelve hours each way, we didn't have a detailed plan, we didn't have tickets to the game, but we went and we had a blast. While we were there we went to a Playboy party, met tons of people, and even ended up getting seats to the game. It was awesome. My girls could have easily chickened out and said it wasn't thought out well enough; what if the car broke down? What if all the hotels were booked up? What if we didn't get tickets? What if all the events were sold out? But they didn't. We took the chance and everything worked out fine. Now we have some irreplaceable memories that will last us a lifetime. *Taking chances, going against the crowd and doing things out of the ordinary is what life is all about. Those impromptu decisions make life stimulating. I always make it a point to do what I want to do even if I am the only one doing it. They say that on your death bed it's not the things that you did that you end up regretting, but the things that you didn't do.* Two hours before it was time to leave New Orleans, Lexima said that she was about to go to the mall with a guy that she just met. I know how we women can get sidetracked in malls, so I told her that there was no way she was going to make it back in less than two hours…but she did. With ten minutes to spare she hopped in the car where we were waiting with the engine running. She had her new purchases which amounted to $3,500 in less than two hours without giving it up. *That's my girl! Birds of a feather flock together.*

…He has a huge ego

Most guys are built with huge egos and a competitive personality; they always want to outdo the other guy. Believe it or not, at times his ego can actually work in *your* favor. I remember a guy that I was having dinner with saw my Chanel shoes. He asked which guy bought that for me, then said he was going to upgrade me. He immediately called up the Chanel store and told the sales representative that he was sending in a special friend and she should help me pick out a nice pair of shoes and a purse to match. After dinner I went to the store and found some shoes that I loved. I took a picture of the pair with my cell phone and sent it to him. He texted back saying,

"Don't get those ones; get the gold ones that are in the display window."

I was furious. How could he tell me to pick out something that I like and when I finally did, then he tells me to get something else instead? I was upset until I saw the price tag of the one he picked. It was double the amount of the one that I picked out...I can appreciate a guy with that type of ego.

POSERS and PREACHERS

Posers are guys who flash their money in public, ride slow on their over-sized rims and cruise with their rented Lamborghini doors open as if they're parading in a car show. They blast their music to the max because they have to be noticed. Their behavior screams: 'I have a little money, come and take it'. Here lies the dilemma. When it's time to dish out the funds the *Posers* put up a struggle. *Wasn't the reason they candy painted their car, and put diamonds in their mouth to attract women who want money in the first place?* Some guys *invest* all their money in putting diamonds in their mouths and now they can't afford to eat. If you look closely at their wad of cash you may be surprised, sometimes it's all one-dollar bills and the only hundred-dollar bill that they have is on top of their stack. I'm sure that they would love to spend some of their money on women, but for many of them the fact is that it's their rent money that they're flossing. It's just an image they work hard to portray.

Preachers are the second type to steer clear of. They want to preach about love and long-term relationships. They say money isn't important and it's the inside that counts. All that is nice, but when they see me hopping out of my Benz, sporting my D&G bag and Prada frames, they feel so compelled to come up to me and ask how can they get a woman like me? Isn't that funny? If they think that money isn't so important then why aren't they attracted to the broke-looking woman? *98% of these preacher types who preach about how insignificant money is, only do so because they are broke.*

PAPER or PLASTIC

It's OK to wear brand names and designer labels because they are tools of the trade, but you have to go about it in a smart fashion. Don't use your money on expensive materialistic things. If a guy wants to spend his money on those items for you then that's perfect, but still rules apply. If he uses his credit card (*plastic)* to purchase it, wisely choose something that you really like because you are allowed to keep it. However, if he uses cash (*paper*) then find the most expensive items in the store because the wise thing to do is to return those items. It's funny when guys ask me if I want to try on the items that they are about to purchase for me, my answer is usually "No, I already know my size." I don't waste my time trying on clothes because I know that I'm going to return it, to get the cash and deposit it in my investment account. *I encourage you to do the same, just make sure to get the receipt.* As soon as you get the cash back *invest* it in mutual funds or bonds. At the end of the day purses and shoes may make you feel good temporarily but you'll feel even better knowing that your money is growing and soon your future will be secured. *I talk about some investment options in Chapter Nine.*

Lesson: #45. *If a celebrity asks you if you know who they are, act like you don't even if you do, after that they may feel the need to prove a point or impress you.*

A few years ago I heard about a huge birthday party for a DJ in south Florida, the party was called "The Temple" and it took place at Club Mansion. At the last minute I decided to go. While standing at the bar, just as I finished my drink a guy with a vaguely familiar face came up to me and offered me another drink. I told him:

"No thanks, I'm good."

He ordered a drink for himself and then he was about to walk away. I stopped him and said,

"Actually, I'll have some sparkling water,"

So he ordered me one. I decided to accept the drink because I realized that by saying no to it he thought that I wasn't interested in conversation also, when in fact I was. Once I accepted the drink we started talking. A couple of minutes later he asked if I would dance with him and I politely said no. Jokingly, I told him that I love guys watching me dance, wishing they can get up on all this. However, getting sweaty and having a guy grinding on me, trying to get his drinks worth really wasn't my thing. We both laughed out loud. Moments later he asked me if I ever heard of a well-known DJ named: Kay (*we'll call him Kay to protect his identity). I told him that the name sounds a bit familiar, and he said:

"Well, that's me"

He extended his hand and asked,

"So will you dance with me now?"

I looked him straight in the eye and said,

"Nothing is going to change."

He was shocked, but he got over it and we are cool with each other to this day.

Lesson: #46. ***Get business cards made so you can slip it to your target in case you don't have a chance to carry on a conversation.***

Some of the best opportunities go by in only a split second. Plus it will make you seem as if you have a lot going on for yourself. If you don't have a business, just get a card designed with your photo and contact info on it. Which brings me to my next point: *Don't dig for gold in only one goldmine.* If you are out on a date and you see another guy that has potential don't allow your date to stop you from getting his phone number. Ask the waitress to give him your card or discreetly signal him to meet you near the restroom and take his number there.

There are guys out there that don't mind if you are not sleeping with them. The only thing that matters to him is that his friends and everyone else thinks that he is getting some action. He'll want to hold your hand, touch you constantly, or even ask you to kiss him. Don't do it! Public

Displays of Affection (PDAs) bring your *stocks* down because by-standers may think that you are taken. Make sure your target doesn't cuddle or hug you in public; remember that you have to always seem available or accessible for other potential targets.

THE NEXT CHAPTER COVERS:

"Subliminal" Technique

Golden Occupations

How to Administer the "Cheap Test"

Some Signs That He's Cheap

How to Get In VIP with Ease

How to Stand Out

Chapter 6

DRASTIC TIMES, DRASTIC MEASURES

...Don't leave your future up to chance.

You can play a major part in creating your destiny.

Drastic Times, Drastic Measures

Money and opportunities are all around you, you just have to know where to look. Most of the time, you won't find the wealthy in a loud smoky club late at night. You have to put yourself in the right environment. If you network correctly you will begin meeting people that will open doors and take you closer to your GOALs.

Yard sales are a great undercover way to scout out a nice neighborhood. Just look online for upcoming sales in the nicer areas (on Craigslist.com you can even select specific communities). Who knows who you may meet? If it's one particular guy that you have in mind then find out his daily schedule. You may "accidentally" get lost in his neighborhood or office building. *Don't worry it's not stalking.* Find out where he goes to lunch or if you are bold enough then set up a business meeting with him as a potential client. *The older, the "golder."* Some guys get better with age, like fine wine. Most are finished playing mind games and most importantly have the mindset and finances to be way more generous. Don't worry about his age because it's not like you plan on marrying him. It's the digits in his bank account you should be more concerned with. There are all types of devices that you can use to get his financial information, like software for his PC that captures pictures of each website that he visits. *I found that out by watching an episode of The Tyra Banks show where she featured intriguing spy gadgets and interesting websites like SpyChest.com.* I'm not telling you to do anything illegal like tamper with his accounts, just take a look. If you don't happen to find any bank statements floating around the place then this is the way to go. *Some guys will leave their bank statements in plain view in hopes of impressing you. If you found it too easily assume that it has been altered. Ignore it!*

<u>Lesson: #47.</u> *When a guy gives you something or grants you a favor you must assume that he wants something in return. In his mind nothing is free.*

He may not come right out and say it, but he may insinuate it. For example, if he agrees to give you money but he wants to give it to you in person, especially late at night, at his place, a hotel, or another secluded location...don't fall for it. *Just because he wants something doesn't mean you have to give it to him.* That's why there are wire transfers and millions of bank branches; all he needs is your name and account number. If it's someone that you just met and you don't want him to know your real name, then have him send the money through Western Union with a test question. As long as you know the answer to the test question, he can send it under any name without you showing identification.

<u>Lesson: #48.</u> *Studies show that people are more than likely to grant requests on Fridays. Maybe because it's payday or the end of the workweek and most people are typically in a happier mood.*

"SUBLIMINAL" TECHNIQUE

Knowing the perfect time to ask for something is *very* important, but sometimes just asking isn't enough. I'm talking about giving *subliminal messages*– not to be confused with "hint dropping."

A subliminal message is a message that's embedded; it's intended to pass beneath the normal limits of a person's perception. These messages are undetected by the conscious mind, but are capable of affecting the subconscious mind which can control the following thoughts and actions.

Sometimes by speaking out loud guys feel like you are *telling* them what to do and the testosterone in them may make them slightly rebel *(remember the categorizing technique discussed in Chapter One when using this tactic).* I'm talking about subconsciously putting it into their minds, just subtle enough for them to think that they came up with the idea all by themselves. For instance:

A. If you're walking in a mall with a guy and you see an outfit in a store window, stop abruptly and gaze at it for a few seconds then continue walking, but don't say a word.

B. While he is right beside you try on that necklace that you've been wanting (even ask him to close the clasp around your neck). Admire it in the mirror then give it right back to the sales representative.

C. If there is something that you like in a catalog, turn to that page and slyly leave it within his vision.
If he's into you, he may ask you if you like the item or even offer to buy it for you. If he doesn't offer to buy it, it doesn't

mean that he hasn't noticed or he isn't thinking about it. As long as it's in his mind then there is a possibility that he'll get the item (even if on a later day like your birthday). This technique works more efficiently if a third party states that something looks good on you, while both of you are present.

Speaking of birthday, I have a girlfriend that always tells guys that her birthday is a week away so they can give her a gift. If you are considering doing that, then make sure you know that horoscope sign of the date you pick.

Lesson: #49. **One of the most successful subliminal methods is music.**

D. Make a CD of songs that talk about wining and dining, going to the spa, getting your hair and nails done, receiving lavish gifts, flying to exotic destinations, and just spoiling and pampering women in general and play it when he comes around. You'll be surprised how people in general buy into that kind of subliminal marketing and advertising. Before you know it, he's competing with the artist and trying to buy you the same things and take you to the same places. *Don't act like you don't know, you know how hyped you get when you hear T.I's "What Ever You Like."*

GD Mix

Feel Like a Woman - Mary J Blige

Here I Am - Nelly & Rick Ross

Get This Money - Jamie Foxx

Can't Help But Wait - Trey songs

Shawty is a Ten - The Dream

Throw It in the Bag - Fabulous

Ain't Trick'N If You Got It - Mullage

I Know What Them Girls Like - Ludacris

Baby By Me - 50 cent

Upgrade You - Beyonce & Jay Z

<u>GOLDEN OCCUPATIONS</u>

If you don't like the idea of working a nine-to-five job because you think you'll just be making your boss richer consider the following. Working for someone else can be one of the easiest ways to gain access to the type of guy that you are seeking (without unmasking your true intentions).

- Be a **bank teller** in an upscale neighborhood, that way he cannot lie about how much money he has.

- Work at a casino as a **cocktail waitress** or a card dealer because most people who visit casinos intend to spend money and tip well.

- Be a **concierge** at a five-star hotel where celebrities and CEOs frequently visit.

- Being a **cashier** in a high-end boutique isn't a bad idea either; the first time your M&M comes in he may be with a woman, but if you leave a good impression don't be surprised if he pops back in your store all by himself.

- If you are looking for a job where you can make some quick cash, try **bottle-service** in a trendy fast-paced nightclub. You'd sell bottles of liquor in the VIP section and make $50 (at the very least) from each bottle purchased. Most people in VIP are going to buy bottles anyway, plus this position gives you the opportunity to mix and mingle with your target without your true motives being detected.

 - **Bartending** is a job with great potential, but you have to select a lucrative atmosphere; a mature clientele is ideal because they usually tip well. Pick a lounge or hotel, not necessarily a club where you have to scream over the music and breathe in cigarette smoke all night.

- Being a **waitress** is the oldest undercover job in the book. *A lot of waitresses meet actors while waiting tables and a lot of actresses were waiting tables before they made it big in Hollywood.* This choice gives you access to people that you would have never otherwise met...after all everyone has to eat. Waitressing is one of the trickiest jobs, because not only do you have to select the right neighborhood, but the time of year and even the shift that you select factor in.

So even though a job may not pay that much, you can still strike *gold* by working there if you network correctly. Waitressing is a bit tricky though because *location* isn't the only factor that you have to take into consideration. You also have to factor in *timing,* because even in the upmost upscale communities there are slow periods throughout the day and each phase of the day brings in different characters.

I don't recommend that you make a career out of any of the jobs that were suggested. The wise thing to do is get an education so you can have a lasting career or open your own business and hire capable, dependable employees. These jobs are mere jumpstarts; you'd only have to work there for a few months, after that you can leave. If you learned anything from me, then you should have retrieved enough contacts from all walks of life and each continent. You can thrive off of them for the next couple of years (while you put yourself through school or secure a higher position at your "real" job).

Note: If your stash runs low don't hesitate to repeat the process.

<u>Lesson: #50.</u> *If you want to a guy to give you money then you have to make it easy for him.*

I'd suggest opening accounts with multiple banks, just as long as you're not being charged a monthly maintenance fee. Try to use banks that have locations in most states, like Bank of America or Citibank. The guys that you meet will more than likely bank with one of those institutions. By banking at the same institution as he does, all he has to do is transfer funds from his bank account directly to yours, in most cases that can be done over the phone.

There are so many things that you can incorporate in your daily routine that will give you access to guys without trying too hard...

- Be selective with your gas pumps. Always get a pump on the outside, on the end closest to the street, so that guys driving by can see you.

- Avoid tinting your car windows. If your windows are tinted then drive with one window down so it's easier to hear if a guy tries talk to you when you pull up to traffic lights. *As hard as you work to pay your car note each month, you deserve to be seen.*

- Get a second line which is only a voicemail (usually it costs $10 a month). Then put a "for sale" sign on your car and list that phone number on it. If you come across a guy that peaks your interest while you are driving and you can't stop, then just point to the sign. *I call this method speed-dating.*

- If you have a business, then get a magnetic sign promoting your business and put it on the side of your car. After business hours forward the business line to your cell phone and you may be surprised how many calls you get while stuck in traffic… just to see if you are the one that's going to answer the phone. *Don't worry, they're easily removable and they won't damage your vehicle.*

… Hollywood, Here I come

One day while still living in Florida I got the bright idea to move to Hollywood. I had never been there before and I only knew one person that resided there. I told two girlfriends about the idea and they said that they wanted to come along. Our plan was to pack our things in my car and just take that thirty-six hour drive across the country. When the day actually came they chickened out. *I was disappointed, but I really couldn't blame them because it was a crazy idea.* However, I was already packed and I envisioned being in Hollywood, so I made up my mind that I was going with or without them. *Most people would find that unusual especially for a woman, but I am perfectly fine being in my own company and taking the initiative to do things on my own. Not much fazes me; I'm a composed individual, and I'm not afraid of taking risks.* I loaded up on Red Bulls, changed my tires, got a tune-up, gassed up my car, and off I went.

It took me fourteen hours just to drive through Texas. In some states it was just open plains, and in other states I was surrounded by mountains. Being able to see the sun rise and set while watching the sky change from sky blue to hues of aqua and from lavender to shades of amber was breathtaking. The time to myself was just what I needed because I was able to gather my thoughts. That road trip gave me a whole new perspective on life and it gave me hope. The whole drive there I listened to music, called everyone in my cell phone and thought about all the things I would do when I made it to Hollywood. I had a long list of things to do, places to visit, and people to meet. I arrived safe and set out to accomplish my tasks. There were some hurdles that I had to get over, but overall everything worked out fine. I remained focused, and was blessed enough to meet the right people who helped me make a smooth transition. *That was my first road trip by myself and I've been driving ever since. It relaxes me and re-energizes my mind. Actually I get my best ideas when I'm behind the wheel. I've even blogged while driving many times; check out the videos on www.Youtube.com/HeyThereBuddyBJ.*

..."Bahama Mama"

I frequently vacation in the Bahamas. Last time I went there with my *SD* and after my photo-shoot he took me shopping. When we finished shopping he gave me about $4,000 pocket money for the day. He made it clear that was all I was going to get for the day, so I should spend it wisely.

Lesson: #51. It is imperative to have a pre-written and researched list because you never know when the opportunity may arise for you to get one of those items.

On the way to the car, I spotted a Gucci store and I screamed,

"I didn't know they have Gucci here!"

I went on and on about how he didn't give me anything for my birthday. He told me that my birthday passed three months ago, so I told him that was the first time I saw him since my birthday so it didn't matter. *I'm always prepared. I previously went on Gucci's site and knew exactly what items I wanted, I even had the item numbers stored in the memo section of my cell phone.* He remained adamant about his decision and told me that if I went in the store I was on my own because he already gave me my daily allowance.

Lesson: #52. **_When all else fails, resort to whining (in a cute, feminine way of course), because most guys will agree to just about anything to shut you up._**

I continued debating with him and told him that the items were the cheapest that I'd ever seen them, until finally he said,

"Let me see what you're talking about."

Once he agreed to go in the store, I knew I had him. When we went inside, he took a quick look around and said that he didn't see any "sale signs," but by then it was too late *of course.* By the time he finished doing his 360- degree turn, I already had the items of desire in my hands and was proceeding to the cash register. Needless to say, he swiped his card.

...the cheap test

It is mind boggling when some people try to make me see that it's ok to be with a guy who is broke or has nothing going on for himself. Seriously speaking, what he has in his pockets reveals a lot about his mentality. When I meet guys that want to take me out on a date and they have to dig in all four pockets and count coins or ask if we can split the bill, I know that something is obviously not connecting in their heads. If nothing is wrong with them physically, then why are they broke still? At 30 years of age why don't they have a car, a good job, or a job...period? I've come to a few conclusions. Besides the current state of the economy, most guys that are in a bad financial situation are because:

1. They decided not to pursue higher education, for whatever reason.

2. They can't get a good job because they've been to jail, - which is more than likely because of a poor decision on their end.

3. Most of their paycheck goes to child support - from having multiple children with multiple women.

4. They're scared of success or commitment.

5. They're lazy.

6. They're just bad-lucked.

Either way I don't need to be associated with any of that mess, because I made huge sacrifices and they can also if they wanted a better life.

Just last week I was out shopping when a guy came up to me and disturbed my shopping session, just to ask me for my phone number. I flat out told him to pay for the items that I was about to purchase. He told me that he didn't have any money. I laughed then asked him why he would try to pick up a woman if he had nothing to offer.

He stared at me in disbelief. What did he think was going to happen? I'm a grown woman, and I know what I want. I don't have time to waste with guys who aren't bringing anything to the table and neither should you.

HOW TO ADMINISTER THE "CHEAP TEST"

Lesson: #53. *On your first date is the best time to administer the "Cheap Test." It's best to know right away what you're dealing with, to avoid any surprises in the future.*

Some men do not believe in spending money on a woman at all, and they have no problems telling you so if the subject is brought up. By administering the "Cheap Test" you'll avoid the guessing work and get straight to the point. When you first meet a man, he'll probably ask you the opening question: what kind of men do you like. This is your opportunity to find out what type of man he *really* is. If he's cheap, won't spend money on a woman unless she gives *IT* up, or just doesn't have any money to spend; it's best that you know upfront, so that you can decide how much of your time you'll set aside for him…or not.

If he doesn't ask you the opening question, then feel free to ask him what he is looking for in a woman. Naturally, after he's answered, he'll more than likely ask the question. Once he asks you what you are looking for, tell him things that are important to most women like: being respectful, honest and spontaneous. Just make sure that the last thing you mention is generosity; you have to make it very clear to him that you like to be spoiled and you can't tolerate a cheap man. After you've listed that last requirement just stay silent and pay close attention to his response. If that approach is too direct for you then just tell him a story of a guy that you previously went on a date with and how cheap the guy was and how much it turned you off. If he asks you what you mean by "cheap" or if he tries to justify stinginess, then it's a very good chance that he may not be able to do a great deal for you financially. If he starts talking about generosity being a two-way street or he'd spoil you if you were his woman, *watch out* because he's expecting you to *put out.*

Lesson: #54. _If you have to pay for your own gas or parking to meet a guy for a dinner date, then it probably amounts to the same as paying for the meal yourself._

If you are too shy to ask to be compensated for parking, you shouldn't have your date meet you inside of the restaurant, but rather outside, in the parking area so he'll have the opportunity to pay the fee. If you'd like for him to pay for gas, but you don't quite know how to ask then try this approach. The next time he wants to take you on a date just follow him in your car. Make sure you tell him that you have to stop at the gas station for gas. If he doesn't offer to pay for your gas when you both get to the pump, ditch him because that's already sign #1 that he's cheap.

SOME SIGNS THAT HE'S CHEAP

- He doesn't offer to pay for something that you picked up and proceeded to the cash register with.

- He keeps a cup, a jar or a bag of pennies.

- He always has a coupon for every place that he brings you on a date.

- He always complains that you never finished your food.

- He always asks for a doggy bag. (*Ps. It's ok for you to, but not him*)

- He eats the food you left when you're on a date.

- He doesn't give you the option to order desert when the waitress asks.

- He repeats the amount of the bill in disbelief.

- He goes to the restroom as soon as the bill arrives.

- He suggests that you split the bill.

If you see any of these signs, then he definitely has the cheap disease - *Save yourself while you still can.*

Lesson: #55. *Always have enough money to cover your order even if he says he's going to pay…just in case he changes his mind.*

...Sir Speedy

Lesson: #56. Beware of fast-talkers; they skip to the next subject quickly so that you don't have time to analyze what they are saying, which is usually lies.

I recall an incident that occurred while I was hanging out on Ocean Drive in Miami with my friend Lacy. We met an older guy that claimed he owned some condos in the area. Since the first moment we met, he was a fast-talker. *Let's call him Sir Speedy.* I had a feeling that he was up to something but I couldn't quite put my finger on it. We told him that we were about to go and get something to eat. He bragged that he knew all the best restaurants in the area and he offered to take us to the closest one. I must admit that the restaurant he chose was quite posh; it was a block from the ocean and it had a relaxing ambiance. We ordered, ate, drank a few glasses of Merlot and talked for a while. He led the conversation, it was mostly about what he had, owned, and did.

Lesson: #57. Sit back and let the guy do most of the talking, sometimes he'll dig himself in a bigger hole without even realizing it. Most guys start lying, start talking about themselves too much, or bring up sex way too early.

When the waitress brought the bill out Sir Speedy's eyes drifted our way. Immediately I recognized what was taking place, so I asked him if he wasn't going to take care of the bill. He said that he just gave a homeless person on the street $200 which was all the money that he had on him. He said besides that, he only ordered an appetizer and had a small piece of my steak. *When I first spotted him earlier that day I saw him withdrawing money from an ATM, so I knew he was lying to me. Come on, who gives a homeless guy all their money and as a result they can't pay for their own meal?* This dude was insulting my intelligence; he obviously had no idea who he was dealing with.

Lesson: #58. *Prepare code signs, gestures, symbols, and words that you can use among your girlfriends in case you are ever caught in a sticky situation.*

I wanted to walk out of the restaurant right then and there, but I didn't want to cause a scene or give him the least bit of a hint. *If he knew that I was planning on leaving, he could have left the table first and stuck me with the bill.* That was a small problem compared to the next problem that I had to face. The biggest problem was that I had Lacy with me. How was I going to give her an indication that we needed to leave *now* without him catching my drift?

Lesson: #59. *The element of surprise is always the best tactic. If the guy doesn't have a clue about what's going on then he won't have a chance to react. By the time he figures it out, it will be too late.*

I quickly conjured up a get-a-way plan. I acted as if everything was cool and told him that I'd be right back because I had to run to the ATM. I purposely left my cell phone on the table. When I got to the door I asked Lacy to bring my phone because I had to make a "really quick" call.

The words: "really quick" was a code we previously made up - it meant we needed to leave NOW. She caught on very quickly. She grabbed her purse, and brought me the cell phone; we were out. *This is why I pick my associates wisely;* Needless to say, we had absolutely no intentions of returning. Sir Speedy kept calling my phone saying that the restaurant was going to press charges, I know he was just bluffing though so I kept sending his calls to voicemail; in one of his voicemails he said that if I didn't have the money that I should have told him and he could have had a buddy of his drop off some cash. *He should have asked his buddy to do that in the first place since he ordered the appetizer– did he expect me to pay for his portion also?* I had the money but I didn't like the idea of him trying to get over on me.

...No Wheels, No Problem

If you don't have a car yet, don't panic because there is still hope. I remember the days when I had to take a total of three buses to get to school...and the trip was three hours each way! Believe it or not, before I had a car I still was able to meet a lot of guys. Ironically, I met most of them while I was waiting for a bus at the bus-stop, including an attorney that came in handy many times. They all spotted me while they were driving by. It's mostly about how you dress and separate yourself from the crowd (literally). It's your duty to stand out wherever you are. If you are a woman who is embarrassed about the car that you drive, then ride with a girlfriend, arrange to be picked up and dropped off or park around the corner from your destination. When it's time to go home, just make sure that you leave before everyone else does. If you're going on a date, just arrive ahead of schedule so that he doesn't have to see you drive up. When your date is over and he asks you if he can walk you to your car, politely decline. Trust me, I know how you feel.

One of my first cars was a Pontiac Sunbird, it was about ten years old when I bought it and it was a five speed manual shift. At the time I didn't know how to drive a stick, but since the car was only $650, I quickly learned. It was a dull red and the trunk couldn't close because I accidentally reversed in a gate. It was missing a hub cap and the lining from the ceiling constantly fell down - I had to tack it up with thumbtacks. I had no heat or air condition. When it got cold I wrapped a blanket around myself to stay warm and when I had to stop at a red light I'd quickly throw the blanket on the backseat before any other cars pulled up beside me. To top it all off, the driver's side door was stuck shut and I had to climb out the passenger's side, all while trying to look cute (it wasn't an easy task). The car was a mess, but that never stopped me. When I parked around the corner from my destination and walked up the block, I walked like I was on a runway in Milan. I'd make a grand entrance in the building but I was sure to beat the crowd on the way out.

HOW TO GET IN VIP WITH EASE

The trick to getting in VIP if you don't have a wristband is to:

Walk up to the rope with confidence like you belong there-go by yourself, not with your whole entourage of girlfriends. Though it is true that there is **power** in numbers, it doesn't apply to this case.

Lesson: #60. ***Statistics show that guys will approach you quicker when you are by yourself. It's a less intimidating situation so it's the perfect opening for a conversation. They usually ask "Why are you standing over here all by yourself?" then go into their spiel.***

Don't be afraid. Bouncers smell fear and they will be on your trail like a bloodhound at the slightest whiff of the fear pheromone.

Greet the bouncer with an inviting smile and say something that makes him feel like he met you previously, like: "I see you're still looking good", "How are you doing tonight?" "Did you miss me?" or "Did my girls leave already?"

Plan A: Talk to him simultaneously while giving him a seductive handshake. You know the soft lingering one I'm talking about.

If he asks if you know each other, lightly chuckle then say, "You ask me that every time I see you."

If that fails, then use **Plan B**. Tell him you're going back in because you dropped your cell phone inside.

If **Plan B** fails, then resort to **Plan C**. Ask for the head promoter or the manager and in a sweet voice tell him that you're visiting from out of town and that your friend (use a big-name celebrity) recommended this place and you'd like to check it out.

If **Plan C** fails then just abort the mission completely. Remove yourself from that area quickly, because you are now looking like a "bottom feeder" and your *stocks* are going down.

Lesson: #61. *Never linger around the ropes, because by the time you try to get in, the bouncer will already know that you aren't apart of the "in crowd".   If you have to work up the nerves or wait for the right moment, then do it around a corner where you can't be seen.*

Some years ago I went to a new club and was angling my way to get into the VIP section.   When I talked to the bouncer he said that he'd let me in but I would have to take care of him. I told him,

"Hell no, I don't want to go in there that bad!"

I thought he meant sex because in the past I heard stories of women giving security guards sexual favors to get into VIP. A few seconds later he asked me if I knew what he was talking about.

I said,

"I think I do."

He then said,

"I am talking about giving me a couple of dollars."

That was a relief considering the alterative.

Lesson: #62. *When you've reached a wall using your sex appeal, a few dollars can take you further.*

Another time I went to an event and the VIP tickets were sold out. The bouncer told me I needed a wristband to get in the VIP section and he was adamant about not letting me in. I returned five minutes later with a 20-dollar bill. Then said,

"I don't have a wristband but I have this."

I gave him the money simultaneously as I shook his hand and like magic he lifted the ropes.

If I ever have to pay my way in an event, I'm going to find someone in the building to reimburse me. If it's a new venue or a different city, I'll cut myself a little slack for having to pay to get in the first time. However, while I'm in there I'm going to get the promoter's, the bouncer's, and manager's phone number so that the next time I'll have absolutely no problems getting in. I was never the type that had to go out with a group; I never had a problem going out by myself because I knew I would always meet people. Besides, most people hold me back, slow me down and just mess things up. I have certain strategies that I always use because over the years they have proven themselves to be effective. I'm confident they'll work for you also. *As a backup, purchase multicolored paper wristbands at Office Depot or Staples, because it's a good chance that they'll come in handy in getting you in future events.*

HOW TO STAND OUT

Lesson: #63. *You have only one opportunity at making a good impression so make it count.*

...Why blend in when you're born to stand out?

- Practice a firm handshake and a seductive one and know when to use each.

- Walk with **power** and confidence; make the sidewalk your runway.

- Practice a fast, sexy strut and always walk like you know where you are going, even if you don't.

- Make eye contact and project your voice while speaking.

- Never stand with your arms folded because it's a sign of insecurity or may come off that way.

- If you have to be in a line of any sort, always get in the very back or the very front, it's just easier to get noticed that way.

- The same thing applies if you have to take a group photo with numerous people, always go to the extreme end.

- Never arrive on time or with more than one other person. People will notice you more if you are by yourself. *I love to have the girl's night out, but if I'm on a mission then I'm going out by myself.*

- Some people have nervous ticks. It's hard to detect them by yourself so ask a close friend what it is that you do when you are nervous. For example, some women twirl a finger in their hair or fiddle with their jewelry when they feel out of place. It's a dead give-away that you're feeling awkward, so stop it.

- If you are at an event with a group of girlfriends then go your separate ways and just connect with them occasionally or at the end of the night. This will give you a chance to see if guys will lie to your other friends at the same event or if they use the same pick up lines on all women.

CLOSER vs. AGENT

Eventually people may catch on to your techniques, but think of the **GOAL** Digging (GD) game in reference to sports; think of it as a draft. There are so many teams and rookies are recruited every year; therefore, the players are always rotating and being replaced. New recruits will be on your playing field every week so it doesn't matter who catches on to you. If you want to be extra safe just don't play on your home field, play in different cities.

There are many types of women, but only two types that excel at the GD game: The *Closer* and the *Agent*. Both types of women get what they want but there is a huge difference between the two. The *Closer* is straight to the point and she is a no-nonsense kind of woman. Once she gets what she wants she moves on, and she moves quickly. Her only interest is closing the deal and she doesn't plan on dealing with her target again. She's the type that keeps the conversations short, blocks his calls and won't think twice before sending him to voicemail. The **Agent** on the other hand is more approachable and personable; she actually follows up with her victims. So to them, she may come off as caring because she lets them down softly and lets them go slowly. It usually doesn't matter if a guy gets a warning from his friends saying that she is only hanging around him for his money because he doesn't feel used at the end of the day. After being "dug" by an **Agent** most guys haven't even noticed. In fact, on the ride home he'll think that the time he spent with her was well worth it (even though he may have spent way more money than he planned and still got nothing in return). The **Closer** will get what she wants, but on the ride home her victim will think, "*Damn, she got me.*" By then of course, for him it will be too late. I consider myself a **Closer** because I have a very low tolerance for BS. I can't smile when I don't feel like it and I'm not very good at hiding the fact that I'm just not into him; still my way works for me. It pays off more if you can fit the mold of an **Agent** because her persona keeps the door open in case he may still be of some use to her in the future. So work on that personality and charm, but don't be too nice; otherwise your kindness can be mistaken for weakness.

WAYS TO MAKE $

Ways to Make $

You can get paid up to $400 a month to drive your own car. Depending on what city you live in, how populated it is and how many miles you drive per month, big companies will pay you to advertise their business on your car. They can

advertise on your window or wrap your whole car. If you don't have a car, some companies will give you a car wrapped with their advertisement. In that case you wouldn't get paid but you'd get to drive the car for free; your only expense would be gas and auto insurance. *Check out the following website for details:*
www.PaidtoDriveAutoWrapforDetails.com

Ways to Make $$

ATMs, credit card machines, snack machines and other forms of vending machines are a great way to make money while having the flexibility to do what you want to do. If you find a store that needs an ATM machine but they don't already have one, all you have to do is contact an ATM company and let them know. If the store owners decide to have one placed in their store then you get money from each transaction made. (One company that does ATM placement is Automated Financial; you can check them out at www.ATMconnection.com). If you sell a credit card machine to a merchant, every time they process a transaction using that machine, you get paid. With vending and snack machines, once you purchase the machines, all you have to do is find a convenient location to place them in and re-stock them every week or so. Some companies will even re-stock and maintain them for you for a fee. Some good locations for vending machines are schools, churches, car washes and Laundromats.

Ways to Make $$$

My very close friend sent me a random text message the other day telling me that she discovered that people could get a lot of money if they donated a kidney. I almost died laughing. I told her she was crazy to even have the thought cross her mind then I asked her what she would do if the one that she had left ever failed.

Ways to Make $$$$

One woman's trash is another woman's treasure. There are consignment shops that buy gently used clothes, shoes, purses, and accessories. Some stores even specialize in buying designer and vintage items. So go through your closet and get rid of last season's items to make some extra cash.

Ways to Make $$$$$

I've seen women exotic dance for a living and pull trash bags full of money off stage. They have done it for years and even though they never paid taxes, they have nothing to show for it today. If you are a woman in that business because you are putting yourself through school or you have to take care of your family and you can't get a regular job that pays enough to keep you alive, I'm not going to knock your hustle. You are #1; you have to take care of you. If you are already in that business, I'd suggest that you do it in a town outside of where you live. Pick a club where the crowd is more mature and laid back and don't get caught up in drugs or excessive alcohol. Choose the club carefully. Don't pick one where you have to work twice as hard for half the money. If you have never danced before I wouldn't encourage you to start. However, if you go against my advice and are going to do it anyway, then just use it as a stepping-stone and don't make a career out of it. Be smart, it's ten times easier to squander your money when you get paid in cash, so make it a habit to deposit the cash in your bank account daily. Make sure that twenty percent of what you deposit goes into a separate retirement account.

If a guy spends his whole paycheck on a woman just to look at her then who's the dumb one? If you are a woman blessed with nice looks, that's great but just remember it's temporary. Before you know it, you'll get wrinkles and start sagging in places that you never knew existed. Unfortunately, it's the cycle of life. The best advice I can give to you is to use your looks while everything is still intact and your mind while it is at its sharpest to your advantage. Everyone isn't going to have what society considers a "perfect body". Be happy with yourself, because when you are happy and confident it shows. There is a glow that you'll have and a bounce in your step that people will notice and be drawn to. I don't recommend this way, because most women who start down this road end up using drugs or selling their bodies. Most aren't focused enough to do it just to achieve higher goals (like paying off college) then get out of the lifestyle at once.

Ways to Make $$$$$$

I researched some lucrative and legal ways to make money and I came across *Egg donations*. Depending on what state you are in you can get paid $3,000 to $8,000 whenever you donate your eggs. The eggs usually go to families that can't have children of their own mostly because the woman had ovarian cancer. You can do your own research on the internet to get more detailed information. With every situation there are pros and cons; if donating to a family so that they can have the gift of life ever crossed your mind then here is some food for thought. In some states you won't know who the recipient is, so you won't even know if the transplant was successful. Or what if you donated to more than one family and the kids ended up going to the same college and dating? The weirdest part of all would probably be walking down the street one day and seeing a child that looks just like you and not know for sure if it's your child or not?

Ways to Make $$$$$$$

In the past decade the use of online dating sites has sky rocketed. Now there are websites where you can find wealthy men (Sugar Daddies) based on income levels, occupations and even how much they are willing to spend on women (Sugar Babies) each month. Some websites that may intrigue you are SugarDaddie.com, Wealthymen.com, MillionaireMatch.com and SeekingMillionaire.com. You can even set up a profile page stating how much you want your allowance to be per month, e.g., $10,000-$20,000. Use these online services with caution. If you upload a photo on your profile then distort the face. If you find someone interesting then at a later date you can email him a clear photo. Don't use your real name and don't give out your phone number. Don't even use your real email address because they can plug it into Myspace.com and find more information about you (assuming that you are registered on Myspace, Facebook or some other social network).

Yes, those are some unconventional ways to make money but I made it my duty to introduce new options to you, as extreme or unusual as they may be.

THE NEXT CHAPTER COVERS:

How to Delay Sex

How to Dig Safely

Lines to Watch Out for

Ass vs. Asset

GD Rules

Chapter 7

DON'T GET CAUGHT UP

*...Steal his heart, his jewels,
then bounce like a bad check.*

(I don't mean steal his jewels literally.)

Don't Get Caught Up

***Lesson: #64.** Even though withholding information isn't the same as lying, some scenarios are too farfetched.*

It's only a matter of time before guys bring up sex. In your attempts to avoid that discussion, saying that you only like girls doesn't always work, because most men immediately start picturing themselves in the equation. I wouldn't recommend that you say you're a virgin either if you aren't, because soon his competitive side will start imaging how it will feel to be the first one "there". Telling him that you are celibate is more believable. If you want to avoid the sex discussion basically what you'll have to do is TURN HIM OFF.

HOW TO DELAY SEX

***Lesson: #65.** Never tell him that he's going to get "IT".*

Most of the time you'll know when a guy is getting aroused and you feel that he's about to make THE move. There are many signs, like the stretch and yawn technique, (when he'll yawn, stretch his arms, then his arm will land around your neck), or he'll have the temperature very cold in his home so you'll want to cuddle under a blanket. Sometimes it's as easy as looking at his arm for a clue. If his veins are popping out, it's because his heart/blood is pumping more than usual. Translation: He's probably aroused and it's time to get the hell out of dodge (or out of his home where you shouldn't have been in the first place). If he is on his way to meet you, here are a few things you can mention that will totally kill his mood

- Ask him to buy you some Monistat.

- Ask him to pick up some tampons for you from the store.

- Ask him if he has any painkillers for menstrual cramps.

- Tell him you are experiencing PMS.

- Find out what fragrance his mother wears and wear the same kind, it may remind him of her.

- Tell him that you haven't shaved in a very in a long time.

- Tell him that most women are allergic to latex condoms because it's made out of hog-skin. The alternative is condoms that are made out of lambskin (but they don't protect against the spread of STDs).

- Tell him that it's been a while since you had an STD test.

- Wear glitter or shimmer lotion. If a man already has a girlfriend he won't want to touch you, in fear that you'll leave tiny shiny pieces of evidence on him. Watch him stay away from you like a Vampire stays away from garlic.

- If all those fail tell him that you have to shit. (I know it's, vulgar, graphic, and sounds disgusting…that's the point). Make sure you've already got what you wanted from him because after you use those lines you'll automatically get downgraded to the "sister category," or dropped from his address book completely because it will be hard for him to picture you sexually after that. He'll have no harsh feelings towards you after you both have gone your separate ways, because he'll feel like it was his decision; w*orks out for you perfectly.*

Lesson: #66. ***Don't open the can of worms. In other words: never bring up sex, and if he does then change the subject.***

...For Rich or Poor

Some women think that it's safe to date a married man. Besides the moral aspect, I wouldn't recommend it because no matter how strong willed you may be, you run the risk of becoming attached in some way, shape, or form if you're around a person for an extended period of time. Some women fall in that trap, they think that married guys are easier to deal with because they aren't clingy and they aren't constantly calling to see where you're at and who you're with. So some women think that it's a good way to bypass all the stress that comes with relationships. I interviewed a number of women, and some of them said that the most passionate sex they ever had was with a married man. I wonder why that is? Can it be the notion of wanting what they can't have? Or is it the thrill of seeing how far they can go without getting caught? One woman said that married guys would often overcompensate by giving her gifts to assure that his secret was safe. Besides getting a divorce, married guys will do a lot to keep their mistress happy, like the shopping sprees that their wives probably don't get anymore. *Some* would say there isn't much incentive for spoiling his wife because he already has her secured. If you are already involved with a married man, the worst thing that you can ever do is threaten to tell his wife or anyone else for that matter. That can be very dangerous because most guys will do *anything* to protect their comfortable lives and hard-earned money.

Lesson: #67. *_You can't afford to lose your mind._*

There are four things I consider more important than money. One is family, two is my true friends, three is my respect, and four is my mental health. So if you are one that is already caught up with someone else's man, ask yourself if you will be okay if one day he says that he can't see you anymore. No good bye, no one last time, no nothing. If there is a chance that you will not be able to handle it, then get out now. No amount of money or gifts will be worth the emotional strain and stress. Ask yourself: if he's breaking sacred vows that he made to his wife, then why should you believe anything that he tells you. **Newsflash:** *you shouldn't.*

Lesson: #68. *_When you first meet a guy he'll put his best foot forward, so know that you are not meeting him but you are meeting his "representative." Do not believe anything that he says; only time will reveal his true intentions._*

…Don't Get Too Close

When a guy first meets you, he'll make the *most* effort to impress you. He'll take you to dinner, the movies and everywhere your heart desires, if he can afford to. Each moment you spend with him, he'll reveal more personal information about himself. Avoid listening to detailed information about his life at all cost, because detailed information about his life or his life story in general is detrimental to executing your mission. It's detrimental because now you'll start seeing him as a "person" and not a "target." You may even be reluctant to accept money from him if you know he is in a financial bind or going through some sort of economic crisis. You should limit yourself as to how often you see him and when you do, select impersonal activities. In other words: don't make it a movie night at his place, no picnics, no walks in the park, and no gazing at the stars. If you're going to a restaurant make sure it's not a romantic atmosphere. If it is, then bring your laptop or a book with you and tell him you have to get some work done before the morning. At the very least, you can text everyone in your address book. The movie theater is perfect (as long as it's crowded and you're not in the back row), because it's hard to carry on a personal conversation with the loud sound effects filling the room. Comedy shows and plays are also "safe" activities.

…Cover Your Tracks

Lesson: #69. **If you ever use a guy's phone to make a call make sure that you not only erase the number you called, but also block the number by pressing *67 before dialing the 10 digits.**

One time I was at an event mingling and my cell phone died. I asked one of the guys in the building if I could use his phone to make a call, *but I forgot to block the number I was calling from.* The person I called was a guy named Zoe that liked me, but the call went to voicemail. Zoe saw the missed call a few minutes later and called back, but by that time I was already gone. The guy answered Zoe's phone call and told him that I was out there mingling! That was not a good look for me.

Lesson: #70. *Women are stimulated by what they hear and guys are stimulated by what they see.*

With that said, guys are expected to lie because the chance of them getting what they want soars when they tell you what you want to hear. So the worst thing that a guy can say to you when you are feeling vulnerable is "just hear me out" or "let me explain" or "can I just say one thing?" If he does start talking then the best thing you can do is to just walk away. If he calls you let the phone ring and if he leaves a message erase it without even listening to it. If you don't take those measures then you'll start accepting his excuses, feeling sorry for him, and bending your rules. There's a good chance that if you go easy on him then he'll go right back into his old ways– *that's called "transfer of power" and he'll win.*

REVERSE PSCHOLOGY TIPS

- If a guy wants you to take a flight to visit him, act like you are absolutely terrified of flying. When you finally do fly, tell him that it was a major step for you but you did it because you really like him, BUT he really has to make it up to you.

- If you don't have a problem riding in a car with a guy don't let him know that. On the first couple of dates follow him in your car and tell him you have "trust issues," or you find it hard depending on guys. When you do finally ride in his car, he will feel unusually privileged.

- Even if it's a guy you've known for a while and you feel safe bringing him to your home, don't invite him in for a few months. Let him wait in the car. When the day comes that you finally let him inside, he'll be ecstatic.

- If you think he is lying to you about something, ask him a question, wait for him to answer and then stay silent. If he is telling a lie, the silence may make him feel awkward. He'll probably start changing his story or dig himself deeper in a hole. *Silence is Golden.*

- If you want to find out if a guy has been somewhere (e.g., the club) but you feel that he'll lie about it, don't come right out and ask him if he went to the club or not. You have to re-word it and catch him off guard. Begin your conversation with another subject then casually ask, "What time did you leave the club?" or "Dan said he hasn't seen David in weeks, did you see David at the club?"

- If you really want to throw a guy off of your track then buy him a drink, but make sure he's worth it. Trust me, it will blow his mind. After that you won't have to say or do anything else, he'll be intrigued and will open up to you because chances are you are the first woman who did that for him. Plus the fact that it seems that you don't want anything from him will make him want to give you more. You'll spend $7 but you'll get a lot more in return. If you are shy, you can send the waitress to take his drink order, make eye contact so he knows who you are, and have her give him your business card.

HOW TO DIG SAFELY

There are psychotic personality types in each income bracket. In most cases you can't tell if someone has psychological issues just by looking at them, so it's best to take safety measures and put everyone you meet through a screening process.

1. As I mentioned in previous chapters, don't give out your phone number, just take his. Its best that you talk to him a few times first to make sure that he is someone that you really want to have your contact info.

2. When you first meet a guy you should ask him if he ever hit a woman. Sure he can lie about, it but it is better that you ask him and see his reaction or hear his response. If he says he never hit a woman but he

shook or grabbed a woman before, then that's just as bad. Leave him alone.

3. If you plan on hanging with a person more than a couple times, it's probably a good idea to request a background check. *It's only ten dollars or so, and you can get one at any police department.*

4. I highly discourage women from riding in a man's car. There is nothing worse than just wanting to get home but your date decides he's going to make pit-stops all through his neighborhood– *we all know that he's just trying to show you off to all his friends.*

5. If you have to ride with a man or if you're just hanging out with him for the first few times, then text his license plate to a responsible friend. To the untrained eye "409HGD" or any alphanumeric code will look like gibberish, but your designated friend will knows exactly what it means. I'm sure the following morning your friend will keep calling you until you pick up your phone, just to make sure that you're okay. Even if the man you're hanging with seems nice and things and are going fantastic, it's still a good precaution to take; because if things change for the worst you may not have a chance to send that text. *It's better to be safe than sorry.*

6. If you have a picture phone you can take a picture of you both and send it to a close friend. Your date may think that it's a romantic gesture, but you know the real reason behind your action.

7. If you are ever in a situation where things seem fishy or you don't feel safe you can leave forensics behind

(like a strand of your hair under his car seat or your finger prints on the windows) in case something happens to you.

8. Always leave a note or let someone know where you are going.

9. Don't allow a guy to pick you up from your home, especially on the first date. Have him meet you at a friend's house or at a public place instead.

10. Take a self-defense class. Hopefully you'll never have to use it, but it's a great skill to learn just in case. I would recommend kickboxing. I took that class and it was fun and I got in shape at the same time.

11. I'd also suggest that you get a weapon. Some options include a knife, stun gun, pepper spray, or a gun. If you have a quick temper then I suggest you stay away from guns. Someone would have to be within an arm's length of you for you to use a knife or stun gun efficiently. Which brings me to my next point: if your perpetrator is within an arm's reach, then he could easily harm you. So, for most women I'd recommend pepper spray (it's small and can easily be hidden). You can even carry it on your key chain for easy access. If you live by yourself, get a watchdog or *invest* in an alarm system.

12. Get to know your neighbors, you never know if and when you might need them (however, don't disclose the fact that you live alone). If a police officer lives in or patrols your neighborhood get to know him also

A Gold Digger's Guide

because if you're violated he'll respond to the call with more urgency if he knows you personally.

13. I spent some of my adult years in Orlando, Florida, and I encountered guys there who had a bad habit of grabbing women's derrières. To eliminate that, when I had to walk past a group of guys I would face them, stare them in the eye, and walk by slowly just to let them know that I don't tolerate that type of behavior. 99% of the time this worked. For the very few times it didn't work, I'd quickly and loudly put the grabber in his place and he'd apologize. However, there are exceptions to every rule. Depending on how a guy touches or grabs you, you know how to react. If he touches you lightly, feel free to get loud and put him in his place, but if he aggressively smacks your derrière just keep walking, don't look back, don't even acknowledge him because that's the type of lowlife that would actually hit a woman if confronted. Just get security if they're available, that's what they are there for.

LINES TO WATCH OUT FOR

- I love you, (because most of the time they don't mean it).

- You look tense, do you want a massage?

- Can I come inside your place to use your restroom?

- We can just cuddle.

- Nothing is going to change between us, whether we have sex now or later.

- Even though we haven't known each other for long, I'll still respect you after we have sex.

- If you're good to me, I'll be good to you (in other words: If you're good in bed, I'll give you whatever you want).

Don't fall for it. Who do you think he'll try to impress more, the one that gave IT up already or the one that he's anxious to have?

140

WARNING

If you're tempted to give "IT" up to the wrong person or for the wrong reason, then take the following into consideration. There are too many STDs out there to give yourself to someone who doesn't deserve you. One mistake can cost you your life. I can advise you what to do but I can't make you listen, so if you choose to have sex after reading this then use a condom. Make sure that you not only put it on yourself but also put it on correctly (by leaving enough space at the tip of the condom to catch ejaculation). Be sure to inspect his package prior to the act and inspect the condom during sex and after you are finished. Don't forget that some diseases and viruses are not curable, like Herpes and HIV. Some STDs can even be transmitted while a condom is in use, like Crabs and other parasites. HIV has become an epidemic especially in the African American community so be careful and know that you can't tell who has the virus just by looking at them. In most cases, a person who has the virus doesn't even experience symptoms for years, so please get tested. If you are a person who has contracted a disease the best thing to do is to start medication, and tell anyone that you may have passed the disease to, or contracted it from, to get tested ASAP. If you are afraid to tell your partner/s then have a healthcare professional call them.

Lesson: #71. *Novelty condoms like flavored condoms are just that...novelty. If you read the fine print you'll see that most don't protect against STDs.*

ASS vs. ASSET

Guys usually see women good for one thing first and more often than not, one thing only... *ass*. To not be boxed into that category you have to make yourself an *asset*. There are a few ways you can be an *asset* to most guys.

1. ***Offer a service*** that they can utilize...besides sex of course. If you don't have a service to offer, then network with people who do, so that you can send them customers and collect your referral fee. For instance, I know someone that has private jets and I know someone else that sells jet fuel– when I introduce them to each other that equals to automatic cash in my pockets.

2. ***Assume a power position*** (*missionary, doggy style or reverse cowgirl aren't options*). A power position is usually established by owning a business, having a great job, a flourishing career or being a part of a well-known organization.

3. ***Be a woman of substance*** (this is usually ensured through an education, experience or wisdom from your elders).

4. ***Be a woman of value***, and don't forget that your value depreciates with each guy that you have sex with. Value yourself first then others will do the same.

5. ***Be on a Power Player's team,*** find out who the most powerful or influential people in your community are and find a way to be included in their circle.

1, 2, 3, 4, and 5 all amount to: R-E-S-P-E-C-T. When you are respected you don't have to worry about guys taking advantage of you. I have friends in the music industry and friends who own major record labels and music studios, with women usually in and out of these studios all day. They're invited to the recording sessions just as "eye candy" to keep the artists motivated. With me on the other hand, it's a totally different vibe; it's a great feeling being able to hang with the fellows and not feel like a piece of meat. They respect me because they understand how I think. They know that sex is the last thing on my mind and my first priority is making money. So with our motives clarified we can move forward and make money together.

<u>GD RULES</u>

- Do not get caught with this book

- Create a Wish List

- Never bring up sex

- If he brings up sex then change the subject

- Never tell him that he's going to get *"IT"*

- Avoid being on his territory and avoid secluded locations

- Avoid hanging out with him late at night

- Avoid alcohol, but if you do drink then know your limit

Don't Get Caught Up

- Don't do drugs

- Always let someone know where you are going

- Don't stay in the "No Zone" the whole time

- Administer the "Cheap Test" in a timely fashion

- Don't be afraid to ask, the worst he can say is "No"

- Set GOALs

- Construct a plan and set deadlines

- Stay Focused, Stay Positive

- Never Settle

- Read

- Budget, save and invest the money you accumulate

- Share what you've gained, teach what you've learned

- Don't lose sight of your GOALs

- Never lose sight of you

In the next chapter I share some personal stories. They include some guys I've met over the years that have attempted or succeeded on getting over on me.

Chapter 8

SHAME ON YOU!

...Learn from my experiences.

You may fool me once, but you can't fool me twice.

Shame on You!

Don't You Just Hate It When...

- the guy that was standing in line with you outside of the club doesn't even offer to pay your way in, but tries to talk to you after you make it inside?

- a guy acts like he doesn't see you and bumps into you just to say "sorry" and start a conversation?

- a dozen guys come up and talk to you only after the DJ called "last call for alcohol," and now the bar is closed?

- a guy pounces on every girl in the building...and gets dismissed. Then he walks over and tries talk to you?

- a guy asks if he can use your cell phone, and you lend it to him then later that night you get a phone call from him?

By being in the entertainment industry for over six years it was inevitable that some of the people who I've encountered were famous. However because my aim is to have you learn from my experiences without slandering other people, I'll only address these fellows by aliases.

"Phili" Fellow

Lesson: #72. *Guys love a challenge; it's in their nature.*

I grew up with a cousin named Norma; we were like sisters when we lived in Jamaica. Once we were in our teens we ended up living in separate states. A few years ago I went to visit her on campus at Penn State, and that's when I realized just how different we've become. Our style of dressing, our career choice, and our taste in guys differed tremendously. We went out to party one night, and she brought two of her male friends along. *In retrospect, I think I really embarrassed her that night.* The night started off all wrong, first there was a long line and I thought that her friends knew the promoters and could get us in without waiting but I was wrong. I wasn't going to stand in that long line and have my *stocks* go down, so I went to another club around the corner until the line was gone. Second, when the line finally went away and we went into the club they didn't even offer to pay our way in so I was ready to ditch them immediately, but Norma was really into one of the guys so I stuck around. Then there was the last straw. I was dancing by myself, as usual, when the other guy came up behind me, grabbed me by the hips and started grinding on my behind. My catlike reflex kicked in and I smacked him and told him to back the hell up. Norma ran over to me and said that she couldn't believe I smacked him, and now no guy is going to approach me for the rest of the night. She was wrong because that only made them come at me harder.

The Producer

Lesson: #73. *If a guy loves you so much he wants you to move in with him make sure he loves you enough to add your name to the deed.*

One morning I got a call from my girlfriend Nina, she said that she was at a producer's house, he was worth about 60-million dollars and I should come over ASAP. I grabbed one of my CDs and headed over there because I wanted his opinion on a song that I previously recorded. When I got there, he listened to it and gave me some feedback then we began recording a new song and made plans to finish it within the next few days. We made plans to keep in contact through Nina.

Later on that night I went to a social gathering and he happened to be there. We greeted each other with a friendly hug, and then I continued on my way. A few moments later his bodyguard came up to me and said that *The Producer* liked me and wanted my phone number, but I didn't believe him. So I said,

"If he wanted my number he would have asked for it the whole time I was in his studio recording."

The bodyguard insisted that he was telling me the truth. To end our debate, I gave him my business card and walked away with intentions of enjoying the rest of my night.

I got home around 5:30 in the morning. As soon as I stepped in I got a call from the producer. He said that he hoped that I wasn't really good friends with Nina because he liked me way more than he liked her. He went on to say how amazed he was when I walked in the room, and how no woman ever had him in awe like I did. He disclosed that he had been with hundreds of women, and he was tired of that lifestyle and was ready to settle down. He told me that I'm beautiful and sweet, and just the type of woman he'd want to marry. In fact, he swore on his child that we could fly to Vegas and get married first thing the following morning. To prove that he was serious he said that he could put a ring on my finger that very day. When he finally finished giving his speech, I said,

"You know I have a lot of experience with guys, right? You know I have a good head on my shoulders, right? You know I'm not buying any of this bull-crap, right?"

He said he would prove it to me, and I should move into his house immediately. I told him there is no way I would give up my place to move in with a guy (even though he lived in a 12-million dollar mansion with a 20-million dollar yacht floating in the back). He rebutted, saying that I could still keep my place, and he'd pay for it, but the whole idea was ridiculous. Aside from the fact that he was first interested in my girlfriend, the guy didn't even know me. I wasn't about to be his new toy for a week until someone prettier caught his eye. The following day I told Nina about his antics, she said that she didn't think that he was a long-term fit for her anyway, so I should go for it.

__Lesson: #74. Guys are territorial. Take them out of their comfort zone because they feel more dominant in surroundings that they are familiar with.__

It's not wise to move in with a man. If one day you ever decide to cohabitate then get a new place and you both can move in together at the same time.

The producer and I hung out for a couple of months, and he constantly told me that we didn't have to rush into sex (which wasn't my intentions anyway). After a few months of him spending money on me and me not giving in, he stopped calling. *Time reveals all. If he wasn't after sex or wasn't trying to buy me, and he actually wanted to learn more about me as a person then he'd still be around.*

Lesson: #75. If you have a girlfriend that is a go-getter you both may be able to work together, so compare notes and exchange ideas.

A few months later I ran into one of his friends. He told me that the producer told him that he had sex with me and my fee was $500. LMAO, I found it hilarious that he couldn't come up with a better-constructed lie. *Poor thing; It was a desperate attempt to reclaim his manhood, so he didn't look like a sucker to his friends.*

The Import

One day while shopping on Washington Street in Miami, I met a guy named Sam- *he's what I call an import, he doesn't live there but he flies in every couple of months.* He drove past me in his black two-door Bentley, then immediately made a U-turn when he spotted me. He pulled up beside me and signaled for me to come over to his car. I told him to get out of the car because I was not walking over to him. He got out and sparked a conversation. Right before he took off, he said that he had a table at Club Mansion, and because he was in town by himself it would be nice if I met him there. I took his phone number and met up with him at Mansion later on that night.

Lesson: #76.** **When a guy asks you what you would like to do (as far as activities are concerned), tell him to make suggestions first. It gives you the opportunity to gauge where his mind is at, and how much he is willing to impress you.

The following evening we went to dinner. While we were at the dinner table, he was trying to think of things we could do next. He suggested movies, the beach, and bowling. I replied no, no, no. Finally, he asked me what I wanted to do. I started laughing and then said,

"You do not want to know what I want to do."

He kept pressing for me to tell him, so, I asked him the #1 test question; I asked him to name one activity that most women wouldn't turn down.

With a look of uncertainty on his face, he asked,

"Shopping?"

With a huge smile I answered,

"You guessed right."

He said that he didn't oppose picking up a couple of outfits, so off to the boutiques we went. He ended up spending about $2,000 on True Religion and Christian Audigier. The shopping episode lasted only about thirty minutes because I did not try on one single item. I hurried out with the same speed that I went in with; when I was finished, I picked up my bags and gave him a "church hug" goodbye. I told him thanks and that we should do this again another day. I was in a hurry to get home so I could get ready for my next target. The following day, Sam and I went out to dinner again. Now that it was becoming clear to him that I had absolutely no intention of sleeping with him, he asked me if he was only good enough to feed me. I laughed hysterically, because in my mind I was thinking the exact same thought.

Later that night, I met him at Club Mansion…again. He spent another $2,000 buying bottles of liquor just for us. I thought it was a waste of money because there was no way we were going to finish them. However, the **Posers** just insist on flossing. After we finished partying, we stopped for something to eat at The Famous Jerry's Deli, and then I gave him a ride back to his hotel a few blocks away.

When we arrived at his destination, he said that he had something in his room that he wanted to show to me. I told him that I didn't think it was such a good idea for me to go up to his room, especially at five in the morning because people may get the wrong idea. He promised that he wasn't going to try to get in my pants (but I knew better). When he realized that I stood firm by my decision, he asked me how much it would take for me to go to his room with him. I remained silent. I wanted to see just how far he was going to take his outlandish conversation. He started his bid at $1,000 and ended up offering me $10,000. *He was really serious.* I told him to get the hell out of my car because I wasn't for sale. At first, he must have thought I was joking because he remained seated, but as the look on my face escalated from shock to anger he quickly realized just how serious I was, and he got out… fast.

I love making the rules and I love having the upper-hand. I will not sleep with a guy for money; I am just not programmed that way. It's not just blocking the actual act from my mind that would be the challenge, but I'd also have to worry about the possibility of the image resurfacing. Weeks later, I'd probably still be fighting my gag reflexes in order not to vomit from the thought. Besides, most of the guys who offer women money to sleep with them are just…gross. They're the types that snore while awake, have hairy backs, skin tags, stomachs that flop over their boxers, and the combination of discolored teeth and halitosis.
.

Sam called me the following morning apologizing, he said that he had too much to drink and he was sorry for disrespecting me. *By that time he was the last thing on my mind, because I had bigger fish to fry.* That very night I had plans to go out with an NFL player that I met a couple of weeks prior. The "NFLer" and I met up at the Florida Room, (a club inside The Delano, one of Miami's most popular hotels where a lot of international socialites socialize). While there, guess who was also in the VIP section and had a table right across from ours? *Sam: The Import.* He smiled at me, gave me a nod, and sent me a text that read:

"I see how you do it. I need to learn from the master.☺"

 I tried to keep a straight face, but I couldn't help but smile back.

Sam recognizes the hustle. We still bump into each other from time to time and when we do, we give each other a hug and KIM. There's no reason for him to be upset because we both were playing a game. Sometimes you win, sometimes you lose.

<u>*Rap Star*</u>

I met a Rap artist through a girlfriend of mine, and we kept in contact. As the BET Awards approached, I called him and asked him if he was going to be in town for the event. He said he was overseas, but he would be back the day of the event because he actually had to perform at the show. He said we should hang out when he got back, and he wanted to take me to the award show with him. I told him that was okay, so he should just call me on his arrival back to the U.S. When he got back, he sent me a text message stating that he wanted to meet up. I replied telling him that I was busy but I would call him later. I didn't free up until two o' clock in the morning because I was working as a red carpet model for the Annual Producer's Ball. *However, I did leave him a courtesy voice mail saying that I was not going to make it, but we could meet up another time.*

<u>Lesson: #77.</u> *Nothing is open but legs at two o' clock in the morning.*

I called him later that day (which was the same day of the awards) and he didn't pick up his phone, which I kind of expected.

Lesson: #78. ***Always have a backup plan.***

In this situation, my back up happened to be another date to the show. I went to the awards and had a blast. The following day I sent him a text saying that I expected that type of behavior from him. He said I was the one who stood him up first...and he was absolutely right! Why would I meet him at his hotel at two' o clock in the morning knowing I wasn't going to sleep with him? I didn't want to go to the awards show that bad that I would resort to those measures. He told me that he was a platinum recording artist and many women are glad just to be in his presence, so he doesn't need to deal with anyone who's not down with "the program"; I thought neither do I. In my eyes, he was just another brother who happened to get a break, but still had no clue about handling a woman.

Officer Desperado

I was nineteen years old when I had to fill out a police report because my debit card was stolen. The police officer that arrived was an African American male in his forties. We talked for a while and discovered that we were from the same hometown. When it was time for him to leave, he said that he'd give me a call sometime. *He pulled a slick move and got my number off of the police report, but I didn't think that he would actually violate protocol and call me.* Later that week I did get a call from him; he said that he was going to a dinner party with his colleagues from the force and he'd like to take me as his date. I told him that one meal would do nothing for me, but if he filled up my fridge *then* I might consider going with him. Well, he filled it up, but when the day of the function arrived I still didn't go. I decided not to go because Officer Desperado began showing stalker mannerisms. He even popped up at my home unannounced and uninvited. I remember coming home, and he was in my parking lot...just waiting! He claimed that he called me numerous times and didn't get an answer so he decided to come over. *If I didn't answer his call, it was either because I didn't want to speak to him or I simply was not home. So why in the world would he think it was okay to just pop up? He had issues.* After that incident, I did what any woman would do if she were being stalked by a police officer...I threatened to call his sergeant and I haven't heard from him since.

The Investor

You will find that most guys who have large sums of money are ego driven because they are accustomed to women cradling their egos. Prime example, The New York Times described one of my past associates as one of the most successful African American investors in the US. He ran his own financial firm and had offices in numerous cities. His top clients were athletes and entertainers. He had a lot of money but never dressed flashy. In fact, he wore his clothes wrinkled and it wasn't unusual for him to wear his pajamas out in public. He said he did it because he didn't want to advertise the fact that he had money. *Of course, women would still go after him once they found out who he was, and what he did for a living.* From day one, he knew my mindset because I told him that if a guy wasn't doing anything to drastically improve my life then I didn't want anything to do with him. He was shocked that I was so blunt. *It was always hard for me to bite my tongue in to get anything from anyone.*

Lesson: #79. *Never accept personal checks, and make a mental note that even with a business check you may have to wait a couple of days before it clears, (in that time the issuer can still make a stop payment order). There's a service called Telecheck - where you can actually verify if a check is legitimate before you accept it.*

He had one tactic that I caught on to. When it was time for him to cut me a check he would always pick something trivial to argue about just so he could justify not giving me the money. One day I decided that I had enough of his antics and ended all communication with him.

Lesson: #80. *Don't mess up your chances of receiving money out of anger. Be smart. If you feel the need to cut that source off, then do so after the cash has been given to you and you've had a chance to deposit it.*

I couldn't hold it in anymore; my pride simply didn't allow me to. *The Investor* had a habit of telling me that I wouldn't get far in life without him (as if he's God's gift to women).

Lesson: #81. *Don't listen if a guy tells you that you won't make it in life or that you need him, because the only time that's true is when you start believing it.*

Yes, he had money but I'm a self-starter and a risk taker; I figured I'd be just fine without him. I have my health and strength; I am fully capable of holding my own and making my own money…and I do.

Lesson: #82. ***Most of the time you won't have to go looking; you just have to be aware of your surroundings, and be open to receiving opportunities when they come along.***

He was the one who pursued me initially; this is how we met. I had just left a Pizza Rustica pizza shop, and I began walking to my car when I saw a car driving slowly past me. It stopped, and the driver looked back, (either he was lost or he was checking me out). He made a right turn at the corner; I crossed the street and hopped in my car. I waited about thirty seconds before I pulled off, just in case it was my attention that he was trying to get. M*y instincts were right. H*e came my way and passed me again, then he made a right turn at the next corner. I thought either this guy was really, really lost or was really, really trying to get my attention. So this time I cut to the chase, I drove right up to his car and stared at him…he started laughing. He was on a phone call and said to the person on the other line,

"I'll have to call you back because the woman I was just following is now following me."

He hung up the phone and asked,

"Was I that obvious?"

I replied:

"Aaaaahhh, yes."

At that point I took his number.

Over the next few months he was committed to the idea that he was going to make me fall in love with him for him, and not his money. We could have actually gotten along had he not been overly concerned about me taking his money. For me, it wasn't that big of a deal because I already had steady income coming in from various investments, my talent agency, residuals from modeling and acting jobs and from my photos available to be downloaded as wallpapers for cell phones. He was so scared that I was just only around him for his money that he unconsciously pushed me away. He's the most fragile person I ever met; that's probably why he was so successful. His biggest line was: "It's still early; I'm going to give you so much more." Months down the line he was still saying the same thing! *If I'm around any guy for that long of a period, he'd be giving me more too. Needless to say, I aborted that mission.*

Lesson: #83. **Pick your battles wisely. If you hit the jackpot (come across a guy that will not give you money but will show you how to make your own money instead), then don't let him go.**

In hindsight: I invested more time in the guys that gave me a few thousand dollars, and I let *The Investor* slip away because he gave me a hard time. At the time I didn't realize that he could have given me something more valuable, like knowledge. He could have easily showed me how to *invest* on a major scale or how to make an additional 100k a year without lifting a finger.

<u>Lesson: #84.</u> **Associate with positive, business-minded individuals who are constantly striving to reach new GOALs. There's a great chance you'll learn from them just by being around them on a regular basis.**

<u>Reggae Artist</u>

I met a legendary Reggae artist a few years ago. He was coming out of Bank of America, coincidentally and I was going in. He had a dark complexion and his dreads hung down to his waist. He stopped me abruptly and started a conversation. I was just about to tell him that he wasn't my type, but before I could get the words out he introduced himself by name. Immediately bells went off in my head, my uncles were huge fans of his. I quickly took my attitude down a notch because I realized who he was. We went out for brunch and hung out for the rest of the day. The following week he had a concert in Atlanta and he said that he'd take care of my travel arrangements if I wanted to see him perform. I took him up on the offer and flew to Atlanta the day of his show.

While he was performing I stayed backstage. When there was an intermission he came off stage and told me that he wanted me to come on with him when he performed his last song. *He knows that I write music so now he was testing me to see if I could actually perform also, or was I going to back down when I saw thousands of people.* When the time came I went on stage on cue. It was an awesome feeling to not only be able to sing along to the songs that I heard while growing up in Jamaican, but to also share the same stage with a performer that was well respected among my fellow Jamaicans. The performance was definitely tasteful.

***Lesson: #85.** Assume with everything there is a catch, so you're not the one that gets caught up.*

The day *almost* ended without incident. When the show was over, he started coming on to me. I told him that I don't want to waste his time by leading him on in any way. I told him that he still had time to talk to the groupies before they all left. He told me that he flew me to Atlanta because he thought we were going to have "fun". I told him that I did have "fun". Then I asked him if he thought that I was going to have sex with him because he bought me a ticket to Atlanta. Bluntly he responded,

"Yes."

I laughed and told him that it doesn't work like that. *From the way he responded, I knew that it must have been a regular thing for him.* I took a cab to my sister's house (she lived in the same city). I enjoyed the rest of my time in Atlanta. As for him…I haven't called him since.

***Lesson: #86.** Demand respect and set the bar high. Let men work for you because you're worth it.*

The Ractor *(Rapper turned Actor)*

The very first time I went to Los Angeles I met a girl named Cindy who I hung out with quite a bit. One night while we were out we met a guy named Carl. He told us that there was a movie premiere for Miami Vice going on, and it was only a few blocks away. He asked if we wanted to go, simultaneously we both replied,

"Sure."

We were excited because neither of us had been to a movie premiere prior. We thought he had passes to the event but when we arrived we found out that he didn't. It wasn't until we got there that he confessed to us that he had absolutely no idea how any of us were actually going to make it inside. It was time to improvise. *Either we could go back home or we could find an alternative way in.*

The street was full of spectators, everyone one was dressed up and looking fabulous. We were dressed casually in jeans and we stuck out like sore thumbs. We hurried back to the car and slipped into dresses.

Lesson: #87. *Always keep a change of clothes and makeup in your trunk. Don't let a great opportunity pass you by because you aren't dressed for a last minute occasion.*

The movie just finished and all the stars were crossing the street, they were leaving the theatre to go to the banquet area. Carl kept telling us to hurry up because this was the best time to sneak in because all the security's attention was now on the stars and not the spectators. We followed Carl to the back area where the food was being prepared. With our adrenalin pumping, we tried to walk in through the kitchen. A caterer spotted us and told us that we couldn't go in that way, and that we had to use the front entrance like everyone else. I said,

"Ok."

And I began headed back in the direction I came from. Carl told me something that very moment that will stick with me forever. He said,

Lesson: #88. *"Never accept the first NO for a final answer."*

Apply the above lesson to all aspects of your life. For example:

If your bank is charging you an overdraft fee, then ask them to wave the charge.

If they say NO then ask to speak to a supervisor.

If they say that the supervisor is going to tell you the same thing, tell them that you still want to speak to the supervisor.

If your cell phone is about to get disconnected for nonpayment, ask for an extension if the rep says NO, then ask for a supervisor. If the supervisor says NO then threaten to switch cell phone providers.

Remember that to a GD, NO never means NO, it simply means NOT NOW.

Carl then told the caterer that his friends were already in the building and had our tickets, but he couldn't get a hold of them because his phone died. Unfortunately, the caterer remained adamant about the situation. It was clearly time for Plan B. Like mice, we scurried back to the front and while all eyes (including securities') were on the stars, we slipped in through a small opening in one of the gates. I remember a random spectator tried to follow me in, she asked,

"Oh, you're going in through here?"

Then she tried to squeeze through also; I told her she couldn't do that. *I was not going to allow her to blow my cover. Sorry but in times as crucial as that one, it's every woman for her own self.* By this time, Carl was way ahead of us. We were in heels and there was just no way we could have kept up with his fast pace. This guy was on a mission and he had just entered the banquet area when one security guard looked back and saw Cindy squeezing through the gate. Then she walked right up to me, *so now it was obvious that we both snuck in together.* The guard told us that we couldn't go in through there and we had to use the main entrance. That's when I pointed to Carl (who was already through the main entrance and blended in perfectly with the invited guests), and told the guard that we were with him. The guard assumed he belonged there and asked him if he knew us and Carl replied,

"Yea, they're with me."

Luckily, we were allowed to go in. Mission accomplished!

As we approached the main area we slowed down our pace and began blending in. Cindy circled to the left, and I circled to the right, then we met up in the middle and discussed who and what we saw in the room. There were a lot of movie stars in the building, we mingled and networked for about an hour or two. Moments later, Cindy poked me in my ribcage and pointed at a *Rapper turned Actor (Ractor)* who was staring at me. I got upset at her for pointing because she broke one of the most important rules– never make it obvious. I knew all along that *The Ractor* was checking me out. In fact, he was checking me out for the last thirty minutes. I just didn't want him to know that I knew that he was checking me out. Just then, *The Ractor* signaled for me to come over to him, sarcastically I told Cindy that because she liked him so much she should go but I wasn't going to be summoned. *Like a floozy, she walked over to him.*

Lesson: #89. *If a guy has any type of respect for you he will not signal for you to come over to him. He will walk over to you and introduce himself...like a real man should.*

She came back ten minutes later saying that *The Ractor* was about to go to two other clubs and he wanted us to come along. That was a shock to me because he was sitting with two other females. I asked Cindy who they were. She said one was his child's mother and the other was her friend. So I asked her why he would try to pick us up when women were already with him. She was just as confused as I was. It just wouldn't be a good look if we left with them, because if anyone else was actually paying attention to the situation they would have noticed that we walked in alone, not with them. *I didn't want to go.* Cindy pleaded and reminded me of how many missions she accompanied me on in the past, so finally I agreed to go with them.

When we left the premiere everything seemed cool, he even helped us in and out of the SUV but he didn't engage in too much conversation. Surprisingly, the females he was with did all the talking. When we were at the second club I kept going in and out of VIP. Every time I left his section he had

166

a puzzled look on his face, because after all he was probably the highest paid person in the building that night. He must have been wondering where I kept going to. I was implementing my second mission (which was to promote my talent agency on his buzz and on his dime). I didn't care what he thought of me because I had no intention of seeing him after that night. I knew I wasn't going to get anything from him, but I was sure going to milk the situation. I was giving out my business cards to potential models (once again I'm always thinking business).

Lesson: #90. ***Instincts are a combination of intuition and experience; you have instincts for a reason so tune into them.***

At the end of the night we all jumped in his SUV for him to take us back to my car. I was shocked when two intoxicated females jumped in the vehicle and he was cool with it. They were behaving desperate and looked like they were down for anything. Now packed like sardines, they had to sit on each other's lap. At this point I had attitude written all over my face because I refused to drift in the groupie zone. Half way into the drive he asked if we were going back to the hotel with him. Instantly I gave him a crazy look, so he redirected his attention over to Cindy (now that it was evident that I wasn't down with his program). He said he would talk to her because he wasn't going to put up with my attitude. I told him that I had cab fare and he should let me out right then and there. He instructed his driver to pull over in a safe spot and I hopped out as soon as the SUV came to a halt. I had never been happier in my life to hop out of a vehicle. *I never understood how successful guys thought that women owed them something or because they're on TV they think that's a ticket to get into the panties.*

Lesson: #91. **Having sex with a guy will not make him like you; if he didn't like you before sex, he certainly will not like you after.**

The Ractor asked Cindy if she was going with me or was she staying with them. To my surprise, she replied that she had to go with me only because she left her stuff in my car (*translation:* if she had her stuff with her then she would have had no problem having a ménage trios with them). One of the females jumped out and asked me if I was OK, I told her that I was fine, but I'm just not a groupie. She said she could see that I wasn't star-struck, but I could come to her hometown any time and she'd take me shopping. I never did take her up on that offer. As far as Cindy goes that was the last time I hung out with her. I can't have any groupies in my camp bringing my *stocks* down. *If I didn't go against my instincts, I wouldn't have been in that predicament in the first place.*

NFL Casanova

A few years ago a couple of girlfriends and I went on a spontaneous road trip, we ended up at Blue Martini in Tampa, Florida, (basically a watering hole for NFL Players). I entered the building like I owned the establishment and walked straight to the bar to order a drink. Before I had a chance to place my order the bartender told me that two different guys were both sending me a bottle of champagne…just like that. I was impressed because that happened within the first two minutes and I didn't even have a chance to scout the place. *Never underestimate* **the Power of PRESENCE**. I accepted one of the bottles and made a toast to my girls,

"May the only pain we feel, be champagne."

Moments later, one of my girlfriends said that she was going to go over to thank the guy who sent the bottle. I told her absolutely not, because I was the one that he sent the bottle to. Secondly, I felt like she would be falling right into his trap. To most women receiving a bottle is a big thing, but he's an NFL player, buying a bottle of liquor doesn't even begin to put a dent in his wallet. His plan was to send me a bottle expecting me to run over to him and tell him "thanks," just so he could start up a conversation. He just knew that sending me that bottle would ensure him getting my phone number and a dance, maybe more. Boy was he wrong. *He probably made a bet with the other guy who also tried sending a bottle, to see who could bag me first.* I chose not to acknowledge him because a gentleman would have walked over to me.

<u>Lesson: #92.</u> *Don't feel privileged because a guy buys you a drink or even a bottle. That's what they're expected to do; because most only buy you liquor to loosen you up in hopes of getting some.*

After I finished sipping on my drink, I went to the restroom. On my way out guess who I saw in the "hall of desperation"? None other than: *Casanova himself.* *H*e stopped me and introduced himself (like I knew he would). I muttered a casual,

"Thank you."

He then asked me if I would like to dance, but before he could finish the sentence "no" came shooting out of my mouth. He said I was mean. I told him that I wasn't, I just didn't dance with guys in the club, and then I walked off. *I guess he should have interviewed me before he sent that bottle.*

Pimp Daddy

When I first went to LA, I met a guy named Montel. He knew of all the hot events that were taking place and he would frequently introduce me to millionaires. On one occasion, he invited me to a pamper party at a beach house. The party was sponsored by one of his millionaire friends who happened to own resorts all over the world. The pamper parties took place once a month and they were a great success, for the guys who showed up anyway. The women who showed up would get free manicures, pedicures, and massages. There was a chef on spot, and an abundance of liquor. *It was very likely that at the end of the day every guy that was invited was getting laid.* At that time the owner of the house had about eight women living there.

Within an hour of being there the owner walked up to me. He had to be in his sixties. He had long blonde hair, big blue eyes and stood about six feet tall. He started a conversation with me, and within the first five minutes he asked me if I wanted to move in. I told him no. My response surprised him because most women who showed up at his parties would have felt privileged for the invitation to move in. *That was my first and last time at his house.* It is unbelievable how many women sell their souls and are willing to give up one of their most prized possession for a pedicure!

Montel also introduced me to another guy who owned a bank. The banker was African American, medium skin tone, and medium built. We ended up going out for dinner one day. When I spoke with him, I acted as if I didn't have a clue about anything *(the dumb down technique).* I told him that I just moved to LA, and I didn't know anyone there. I also asked him if Montel always introduced him to random women, and he said,

"Yes."

He broke it down for me, and told me how things work, *at least in his world and mind.* He said tons of pretty women come to LA every week and guys who have money (like him) would pay women like me to have a "good time." In other words: Montel was trying to pimp me. *The key word is "trying." He obviously got the wrong 411 on me. I* laughed and told him that it would never happen right before I grabbed my purse and walked out of the restaurant. Later that day I got a call from Montel because the banker told him that I gave him a hard time. Montel told me that I would never make it in LA because I wasn't willing to do what it took. *Fast forward three years later… I'm presently in LA and doing just fine.*

Andrew Jackson

Lesson: #93.   ***You have to look out for yourself.   Test everything.***

Purchase a counterfeit money detecting marker at Staples in case you ever need it.   If a guy buys you jewelry, get it tested by a jeweler or invest in a diamond tester.   If he buys you a "designer" bag then take it to the store and get it inspected to make sure it's the real deal.

When I was in my teens, I took a trip to New York. One day while there, I went in the city to do a little shopping. When I got there, I took the train to my brother's house and then started walking from the train station to his house only a few blocks away. While I was walking a guy approached me and he seemed pretty nice. We spoke for a few minutes, and then he insisted that I should just hop in a cab and he'd pay for it. I agreed. He gave me a $20 bill, printed on it was the famous face of Andrew Jackson and he put me in a cab. When I got to my destination and handed the bill over to the driver; he inspected it and then told me that it wasn't real and handed it back to me. I was flabbergasted. I told him that I didn't have any cash on me, just a debit card and reminding him that he even saw the guy put the money in my hand. He said that he didn't care and that he was going to call 911 if I didn't pay him. *I'm pretty sure having counterfeit currency is a federal offense.   I've been fortunate enough to never have been arrested and I was not trying to go to jail, especially over something that wasn't my fault.* I had a pair of shoes that I just bought in Manhattan and I told the driver to hold on to them while I went to the ATM. A few minutes later I returned with some "real" cash and the driver relinquished my newly purchased stilettos. Imagine what would have happened if I *really* didn't have any money. It was only a $6 cab ride but that ride could have cost me my freedom…All because I trusted a stranger. *You live and you learn…it was then the GD Kit was invented.* (The GD Kit includes multicolored wristbands, a diamond tester, a counterfeit detector pen– and some other top-secret gadgets).

Uncle Fester

A few years ago I had the chance to go to Paris, I was thrilled because it came way sooner than I anticipated. A real estate agent from San Francisco wanted to take me there for a week. That sounded perfect except for one thing: he was overly anxious to get in my pants. I thought that with time he would calm down and stop acting so desperate, but time proved that theory wrong. He reminded me of Uncle Fester from the Adams Family cartoon. He was short, had big gut, a bald head and huge eyes. He continued making sexual advances towards me. I told him that I didn't want to have sex with him, but if I ever changed my mind I would let him know. I also reiterated that if I did end up having sex with him and I wasn't mentally ready, then he would never see me again. *Guess what his response was?* He said it was a chance that he was willing to take. What a creep! He has absolutely no regard for my feelings. I didn't let him see how much his inconsiderate comment disturbed me, but I immediately devised a plan. I met him at the airport to check in an hour before *our* flight left for Paris. He checked in at one counter and I checked in at the other. When it was time to board *our* flight he told me that I was going on the wrong plane. I turned to him, looked straight in his eyes and replied:

"No, I'm not!"

What he failed to realize is that while I was at the check-in counter I changed the destination on my ticket to New York to visit my family instead. I'm sure at the last minute he'll find someone else to hang with in Paris for a week, or maybe not.

The Crypt Keeper

Lesson: #94. **Don't judge a book by the cover.**

Last year I met a fellow from London. He was a Caucasian male, had to be in his sixties. He was about 6'2, had a slightly hunched back, and the middle of his head was shiny due to hair loss. He had a striking similarity to Gargamel (*you know, the sorcerer from the Smurf's cartoon*). I met him on South Beach while on my way to an audition. He approached me and started a conversation. I answered his questions hastily, but still not missing a beat I continued my fast strut. He was considerably older and I really didn't expect him to keep up, but he did. I told him to just give me his business card because I was running late. I took his card, told him that I would give him a call, and I continued on my way. *I wanted to get away from him quickly because I didn't know if chasing women on South Beach was a regular thing for him. If it was, then I didn't want to have anything to do with him.*

Honestly, I had no intentions of ever calling him until I inspected his card. It was a plain white card with no pictures or graphics, just his name and three phone numbers. At first,

I thought that this guy was so cheap that he couldn't afford to have decent business cards made. I took a closer look at the card and there was no occupation on it either, so I suspected that he was a con-artist. Upon further investigation curiosity began setting in because the phone numbers that he listed were for three different countries (the US, Barbados and London). At that point, this peculiar guy had my attention. *Let's call him the Crypt Keeper.* A few weeks later, I did some research and I discovered that he was one of the wealthiest guys that I ever encountered. He was worth a whopping 1.1 billion dollars. He raced horses for a living, not literally, but he owned the horses and had jockeys that rode them. I gave him a call. We spoke for a bit and decided to keep in touch over the phone.

__Lesson: #95.__ When a guy does something big for you don't show too much excitement otherwise he'll feel like his mission is accomplished. Keep him striving to put a smile on your face.

One day he called me up and said that he was going to Paris the following day for a business meeting. He said it would be nice if I could meet him there, so we could do some shopping after his meeting. I told him that I needed an hour to think about it and check my schedule. I called him back in an hour and told him that my schedule was pretty free that week so I'd take him up on the offer. *I was ecstatic on the inside but on the outside I played it cool.*

__Lesson: #96.__ Never have a guy fly you anywhere without it being a roundtrip ticket. You should also require that he gives you enough money for food, transportation, and *accommodations in case something goes wrong (PRIOR to boarding your flight). Just know that if the method of payment is in his name, then he may be able to cancel the ticket at any time.*

The Crypt Keeper told me to buy the plane ticket and he would reimburse me when he met me at the airport. *I thought this guy must be crazy if he thought that I was going to risk losing MY money.* I would be out of $2,000 if I bought the ticket and he did not show up at the airport, or if we just did not get along. I told him absolutely not, but maybe next time. He quickly found a solution and had a friend of his wire the money to my bank account; FYI: I told him that the ticket cost $4,000. *I mastered the art of doubling up.*

<u>Lesson: #97.</u> *Never ask a guy how much of his money you are allowed to spend. Let him stop you. Some of them will even resort to charging it on a credit card if they can't afford it.*

The Crypt Keeper wanted me to get there in the evening, but I thought it over because I know what I am willing and not willing to do. I figured if I get there in the evening all the stores will be closed and who knows what he'll want to try in the night. Instead, I booked a flight that would get there the following morning.

When I arrived I wasted no time to visit the shopping district. We shopped at D&G, Gucci, and LV. I went in the LV store with the intention of getting only one piece of carry-on luggage (which I had on my *Wish List*). The store was huge. It was two stories tall and seemed like it had every single piece of LV luxury item ever manufactured. It even had a LV bed that folded up into a suitcase. *A woman like me could go crazy in a place like that!* I found the piece of luggage that I wanted and proceeded to bring it to the counter. He didn't even look at the price tag (which was a little over $2,000); he was just anxious to swipe his card. So when I saw that money was no problem to him, I quickly grabbed another matching piece. *I like his kind.* When we went in the other stores, he paced around outside while I was inside shopping. He'd pop back in every fifteen minutes or so and when I was ready to cash out, he didn't even flinch. No questions asked.

Lesson: #98. I highly advise against sharing hotel rooms with a guy. Insist that you have your own room with only your name on it and only one key. Have him pay for the room with cash instead of a credit or debit card (so he will not have any say on future changes because his name isn't on the billing information).

When we got back to the hotel, immediately he tried to "cash in." He started rubbing my arm and it's like my skin began to scream. He took a step closer to me and whispered how sexy I was and how badly he wanted me. I took a baby step backwards, because I knew what he wanted and I did not want to give it to him. I began feeling uneasy, and my mind started racing. I was trying to think of ways to steer him off his course. I could have just picked up my bags and walked out of the room but I didn't want to seem like the one dealing out a bad hand of cards. Instead of having sex with him because he bought me some items, I decided to not give up my **power** by refusing to be ruled by guilt. *Basically I* *flipped the script.* After all, I wasn't the bad guy. We never agreed or even discussed if and what he was going to get in return. I stopped him dead in his tracks and deflected his intentions by simply asking him a *"No Question."*

Lesson: #99. *If you feel things getting heated and your target starts coming on to you sexually, then ask a "No Question" in order to get out of the situation. In other words, ask him for something that you know he's going to say "No" to, then let that be your excuse to leave.*

I anxiously blurted out the first thing that came to mind, in hopes that it would throw him off track:

"Will you buy me a new car?"

With a baffled look he said:

"Honey, I don't know you that well yet"

And I responded:

"Exactly! You don't know me that well to rub on me either."

I didn't need a new car, and if he did get me one I still wouldn't have slept with him. It was my way of testing him and more importantly having an excuse to leave without giving it up – all without me being the one at fault. He slept in the bed and I slept on the couch; Instead of staying there for a week as planned, I changed my flight to the first one out that morning. I didn't feel bad because the agreement was to meet him in Paris to go shopping, nothing more, nothing less. He should have interviewed me before he spent close to $20,000. I didn't owe him anything. Besides, even if I were that type of woman, what incentive would I have to lie on my back after I already got the targeted item off my *Wish List* and more?

Lesson: #100. **_You have to recognize the signs early on, because once he starts showing signs of frugality it only gets worse. Be ready to walk away if he isn't willing to agree to your terms. You may be tempted to stay around longer or compromise to get more items… but at what cost? Your GOAL is to not give it up so you have to be strong. Get one item and KIM._**

One of my girlfriends said I should have closed my eyes and took it from the back! She said that it was a bad idea for me to let the Crypt Keeper go and I could have kept him for future use because after all he was a BILLIONAIRE. Well, this is how I see it: if he wasn't willing to give me what I wanted even though he could afford to, then he would only give me more problems in the future. Next thing you know, he'd be writing IOUs. *I don't bend my rules, I don't beg, and I don't barter.* If you remember the following lesson you'll be okay.

Lesson: #101. **_How much he has is not as important as how much he is willing to give._**

…Pop Tags

After applying the *Island Hopping Techniques* you'll be able to travel the world at his expense, and hopefully you'll never

In Paris at the Eiffel Tower

get caught in the following situation. On my way from Paris with all my purchases, *I mean HIS purchases,* Customs got me! They asked me if my items were new purchases and I proudly told them yes. Then they asked me how much did they amount to and I told them. Then they directed me to step out of the line and began questioning me about what I did for a living. They looked at my business card and inspected my website like I was on "America's Most Wanted" list. They went through my bags and calculated the cost of the items then they told me I had to pay $800 dollars in custom fees or they were going to confiscate everything. I was appalled. I tried to explain to them that they were gifts, but because the cost was above the duty free limit, I had to pay up. I wished someone warned me ahead of time because I would have took everything out of the original bags, popped the tags right off and stuffed everything in my suitcase. *They were worrying about the wrong thing; they needed to worry about Bin Laden instead of Dolce & Gabanna.*

To sum it up, I've met a couple bogus guys in my lifetime but I refused to allow them to break me down. They only made me stronger, and smarter.

THE NEXT CHAPTER COVERS:

The Ten Steps to Success

1. Keep Your Credit Clean
2. Choose Assets over Liabilities
3. Create a Budget and Save
4. Buy Insurance
5. Look into Investment Options
6. Stop Renting! Purchase a Home
7. Get an Education
8. Open Your Own Business
9. Read
10. Share What You've Gained

SECTION: III

Take Control of
Your Destiny

Chapter 9

BRING YOUR STOCKS UP
(literally)

...Secure Your Financial Future.

The GD Game is Like Blackjack, you have to know when to cash in. *Get Ready, Get Set, GOAL Dig.*

Bring Your Stocks Up (literally)

THE TEN STEPS TO SUCCESS

I wish I learned the information in this chapter sooner. Please pay extra attention to this chapter because this is the most important portion of this book. Don't wait until years down the line to put this knowledge to use. If you are still in the same financial position five years from now then it's your own fault. I'm sharing valuable information that I've learned over the years with you so ignorance can no longer be your excuse.

Taking money from guys should merely be a hobby, a game, a challenge, something you can do in your spare time. Your first priority should be ***making*** your own money. Over the years this is what I've learned: if you want to attain wealth and more importantly retain it, you have to condition your mind and your way of thinking. A lot of people think that if they won the lotto today most of their problems would be solved. They don't realize that if their mindset stays the same then they'll end up right back where they started. Someone can give a homeless person a million dollars and in a year they'll be right back in the same predicament if they still have that "homeless" mentality. Don't leave your financial future up to chance; instead set GOALs, plan ahead, and map out how you're going to get to your destination. If you still need some reinforcement, consider enrolling in a financial planning course.

KEEP YOUR CREDIT CLEAN

Lesson: #102. ***Without enough cash or good credit in America, you can't get anything.***

Credit can be a wonderful thing if, and only if, you use it responsibly. For most people, that isn't the case. Applying for credit is essentially borrowing money– money that is going to incur interest over time. If you don't have a good plan and a specific time frame in which you are going to pay it back, then I suggest not applying for a line of credit in the first place. If you want to play it safe, only borrow money for a mortgage…anything else can wait until you have enough money saved up. The easiest time for anyone to be approved for a credit card is when they are in college, that's ironic because we all know that most college students are not ready to take on financial responsibilities straight out of high school. As a result, we see a huge problem in society that has spindled out of control. Not only are college students graduating with thousands of dollars in debt due to student loans but credit card debt also.

You may be one of the few people with perfect credit, and for that I commend you. If you are not one of those lucky few, then I would suggest that you take some steps to get your credit in order. The whole concept I am teaching is to get money and make that money work for you in the long run. With that being said, it's impossible to make your money grow if you are in debt. You can find some useful information about bringing your credit score up on www.Equifax.com. They also have a credit watch program, where they'll send an alert to your email every time there is a change on your report. It's $9.99 a month and it's definitely worth it.

Credit scores range from 300 to 800. A good credit score falls between 700 and 800. *Here are some tips you can use to bring your credit score up if necessary.* First things first, order a copy of your credit report from all three credit bureaus to see if you owe anything. You can also view your credit score on www.Fico.com. At first you may be overwhelmed if you owe a lot, but acceptance is the first step, so don't be afraid to face the fear. The three credit bureaus are Experian, Equifax, and Trans Union; Google them to get more information. Once you order and receive your reports, dispute any items that are not yours or that you don't agree with. The creditors have 30 to 45 days to prove that the account is legitimate, and if they fail to do so within the time allotted then in most cases, the negative account is removed from your report.

Secondly, look at the dates of the delinquent accounts. It's best to work on the newest delinquencies first because they impact your credit score more that the old delinquencies do. If you have a credit card that you owe a lot of money on, call the creditor and see if you can work out a payment plan. Once you are able to get it down to a zero balance do not close the account. If you close the account, it will seem as if you don't have that much credit history. Instead, leave it at a zero balance, and just don't use the card again. One trick I learned is to put the credit card in a Ziploc bag, add water and then freeze it. Chances are if you want to use it to make a purchase, by the time the ice melts, you'd have enough time to rethink the purchase and probably end up changing your mind.

A smart strategy to get out of debt is to start paying off the accounts that are incurring the highest interest rates first. If you want your credit score to jump up quickly then ask someone who has a credit card that has been in good standing for years to add you to their account. They don't even have to give you a card; as long as your name is listed on the account it will seem as if you had good credit history for the whole time that account was open. If you are trying to build your credit, you can do it by taking out a secured loan at your bank. You have to have the same amount of money that you are borrowing in your savings account. Just make your payments on time and each month it will be reported to the credit bureau, and as a result will gradually raise your credit score.

There are a few ways the credit system can try to trap you into getting a credit card. **1.** A lot of car rental businesses will not rent a car to you unless the rental is paid with a credit card. Or they may penalize you by charging you a deposit if you pay by debit card. **2.** Many airlines will try to bribe travelers by offering them free flight miles or a free flight if they apply for a credit card.

Lesson: #103. *The more you apply for things and the more your credit is checked, the lower your credit score falls.*

If you feel that you absolutely have to get a credit card then just decide on one. When it's time to get one don't do it off of impulse. Don't just apply because of a commercial on television or because you got a letter in the mail saying that you are preapproved. Evaluate everything...If you travel a lot and you use a specific airline for most of your trips, then you'd probably benefit best by applying for that airline's credit card. If you always shop at a certain department store, then you'd probably want to apply for that store's card. Make sure that you read the fine print information about annual fees etc. and don't sign up for one company until you've compared benefits and interest rates with other companies. Try to shop around for the lowest interest rate possible. **FYI**: The higher your credit score is then the lower your credit card interest rate will be.

CHOOSE ASSETS OVER LIABILITIES

Lesson: #104. Before you purchase an item, take the time to ask yourself: "Is this an asset or a liability?"

Assets vs. liability: In trying to distinguish the difference, remember that assets help you and liabilities hurt you in the long run.   An asset is anything that you own that has exchange value, meaning: you can sell it for a profit at a later date. A liability on the other hand, is anything that puts you in debt or anything that depreciates in value. For example a new car depreciates the minute you drive it off the car lot. So if you bought a brand new car today and sold it next week, you're going to get considerably less than what you actually paid for it. If you are in the market for a luxury car, instead of purchasing one with zero miles, consider getting one that was manufactured in the same year but was previously owned. That will save you some money; besides, what's important to most people is how the car looks, how it drives, or the features it comes with…not necessarily the mileage. The biggest mistake that the poor and middle class make is accumulating liabilities because they think they're assets, so know the difference? For the record: car rims, clothes and jewelry are liabilities.

CREATE A BUDGET AND SAVE

Lesson: #105. ***Never let anyone know how much money you actually have. You always have to have a secret stash that no one knows anything of.***

One major financial mistake that people under thirty years of age make is purchasing depreciating assets (liabilities), such as cars and jewelry. Another major mistake is failing to budget. I would suggest that you collect your receipt for every purchase that you make (no matter how small it is). It is important to keep your receipts because they will help you keep track of the items you spend the most money on. Review your receipts monthly and see if you can cut back on some of your expenses. Get twelve envelopes and write each month on them, then file the receipts accordingly to help you keep track. By doing so it will be easy to pinpoint your biggest purchases so you can find a way to cut back. For example, if your most expensive purchase is gas, then consider getting a motorcycle or scooter instead of a car (you'll cut back on gas and you'll look pretty hot riding it too). Another way you can cut back is by carpooling to school or work, or even using the metro system if it's available in your city. The metro system may not be as luxurious as driving in your own vehicle, but it may be more cost efficient to use public transportation just to get to work or school until you've reached your desired amount of savings. *Think about it this way:* the money you save by not having to purchase gas everyday can go towards the down payment of purchasing your new home or whatever GOAL you have in mind. *Now doesn't that make you feel warm and fuzzy inside?* For motivation rip a check out of your checkbook and write the desired amount you'd like to have saved on it. Keep it in your wallet so every time you open in with intensions of spending, you'll be reminded of your GOAL. Hopefully, one day you'll have that amount in your bank account.

After you pay your monthly bills, past debt, life/disability, and health insurance you may spend some money on yourself for entertainment, personal items, or dining out. However, it is imperative that you set a specific amount of money for each month, and once you've reached that limit you are forbidden to spend another cent. You have to make a conscious effort to put some money away from each time you get paid, before you start to splurge on luxuries, and entertainment. Saving 10 to 20% is ideal– putting money away is only the first step. The second step will be investing that percentage.

BUY INSURANCE

One of the most irresponsible things you can ever do is to not have disability, life, or health insurance (especially if you have people who depend on you). If you don't have health or disability insurance, a good time to start looking into it is now. At this moment, you may be healthy but what would happen to you if you got sick or were in an accident and were no longer into a position to earn income? What would you do if you didn't start saving or investing yet?

Another thing that we all don't like to think about is death, but unfortunately it's inevitable, so don't leave your loved ones with the added burden of funeral expenses. *Invest* in life insurance. A good company is Gerber Life Insurance and (1-800-704-2180). They offer both term life and whole life insurance policies. It's a short sign up process and is very easy to get started.

LOOK INTO INVESTMENT OPTIONS

Lesson: #106. ***A great way to learn about investing is to join an investment club.***

You may think that saving your money is going to get you ahead, sorry to be the bearer of bad news, but it isn't. *Investing* it will. Instead of putting your money in a regular savings account ask your bank about **Money Market Accounts** (MMAs) because in most cases you will receive more interest on it and there are no penalties for making withdrawals. MMAs are safe just like a savings account, but with most banks you can't open one without a minimum of $1,000, (check with your specific bank or credit union for requirements). It's a great way to help you get into the habit of saving your money until you've learned enough about investing, and feel that you're ready to take that step.

Certificates of Deposits (CDs) are saving vehicles (issued by banks) that guarantee a certain percent of interest over a certain period of time usually three, six, or twelve months. As far as the amount of interest that is earned, CDs are a step above mutual funds, but they are still ultra conservative. They are completely safe, and the funds are federally insured. The rate of return depends on the market and economy; the interest rates also vary among banks. The biggest difference between a CD and MMA is that MMAs can be used just like Saving Accounts but with CDs your money is tied up, and making a withdrawal prior to the date agreed upon will result in a penalty or fee. It certainly beats a regular savings account *IF* and only *IF* you are certain you won't need the money for a couple of months.

Bonds are long-term debt instruments, which means that you lend a company, city, state, county, or the federal government money and in exchange they'll pay you a certain amount of interest over a certain amount of time…usually years. Bonds are also very safe and when you purchase them you lock them in at a guaranteed interest rate. If you have a lump sum of money that you want to *invest* long-term and you aren't in a position to take any financial risks, then bonds may be a great option.

Types of bonds include the following:

Treasury bonds are issued by the federal government.
Saving bonds are issued by banks.
Corporate bonds are issued by companies.
Municipal bonds are issued by counties, townships, etc.

Mutual Funds are not federally insured so you run a small risk of losing money. However, those chances aren't great because Mutual Funds consist of not only stocks but low-risk bonds also. Even with the risk of Mutual Funds, most people still earn more interest on their money than a regular savings account or MMA. It usually takes a minimum of $2,500 to start a Mutual Fund but in some cases you can start with as little as $100 if you agree to deposit a minimum of $50 a month into that account. Mutual Funds are way less risky than investing in stocks, and they don't require as much time management either. Your bank can refer you to a financial advisor who sells Mutual Funds. You can also purchase them through insurance agents, accountants or mutual fund super markets such as TD Ameritrade, Vanguard or Fidelity.

TDAmeritrade 1800-669-3900, www.TdAmeritrade.com
Vanguard   1800-997-2798,   www.Vanguard.com
Fidelity   1800-554-9797,   www.Fidelity.com

One of the best ways you can review information on mutual funds is at www.MorningStar.com or you may visit your local library for more information.

Lesson: #107.   *You're never too young to plan your retirement.*

If you are employed, make sure to ask your employer if they have a *401K Plan,* which is a savings account toward your retirement. You may think that you are too young to worry about retirement now, but it's never too early to start planning for your future. If you think that Social Security benefits will be enough to support you when you're retired then think again. I am pretty sure that in forty years Social Security will not exist. Plus, it's just a bad idea to leave your financial future in the hands of the government or anyone else. *Take control; the time is now.*

Unfortunately, it doesn't matter how good looking or smart you may be, you can't hustle forever so use the money that you are accumulating and make it work for you in the future. If you are currently seeking employment, try to apply for a job that offers a 401K plan and ask the company if they'll match your contributions (meaning whatever amount you deposit in your 401K monthly, they will give you the equivalent amount). One good thing about 401K plans is that the contributions come directly out of your paycheck even before the check makes it to your hand, so you will not have a chance to spend it. Best of all, it is tax-free (as long as you don't make a withdrawal before age 59.5 that is). Most people don't realize that truly maximizing tax advantages requires tax planning. There's more to it than just filing your tax returns, you need a good accountant. *The wealthy know that there are many legal ways to avoid heavy taxation, for example, by owning your own business you can "write off" many expenses.*

Lesson: #108. *Accountants look behind, and Financial Advisors look ahead.*

Accountants look at your past financial history and can tell you if you have done anything wrong, and Financial Advisors *invest* and plan for your future.

If you are self-employed then consider opening an *IRA Fund.* It's meant for people with long-term financial GOALs, so don't expect to withdraw money every couple of months. It will be money to live off of when you are retired or just tired of working. Wouldn't it be great to live in a beach house on an exotic island and just sip Piña Coladas with mini umbrellas if you choose to? *Now you get the picture.* Start investing and planning for your future now. The younger you start investing, the more money you'll have when you get to your retirement age.

Lesson: #109. *Never purchase stocks in a company unless you've read their mission statement, done your research, and know exactly what it is the company does and how they operate.*

Stocks aren't so black and white; they fall in a gray category. It can be somewhat of a challenge because there is no set formula that you can follow. You just have to make educated guesses, study the past history of companies and keep a constant eye on the market. You have two ways to make money with stocks:

1. Through capital appreciation. This means selling your shares for a higher price than what you bought them for.

2. Through dividends. This is a piece of the company's profit that is paid out to stockholders.

Stocks are way more risky than Mutual Funds, CDs, and Bonds. Nonetheless, with great risk come great rewards. *Many people make enough off Stocks that they don't have to work.* You can purchase Stocks through a stockbroker or purchase them yourself online. Some websites where you can make purchases include www.Ameritrade.com, www.Scotttrade.com and www.Etrade.com. Most people today find it less expensive to purchase online; you can start with as little as $500. *In some cases even less; TD Ameritrade only charges $10 per trade to purchase Stocks.*

Diversification is a strategy that is used to decrease your chances of losing the money that you *invest*. There are a few different ways to diversify.

1. You can increase the amount of companies you own Stock in.

2. You can select Stocks from various fields of business.

3. You can *invest* in Real Estate and Bonds.

You can find some Stock ideas in The Wall Street Transcript, Barron's, or on BeginnersInvest.About.com & TheStreet.com. Later on in this chapter I list a few books that will give you more detailed information on investing. In the meantime get familiar with the Wall Street Journal and money-conscious magazines like Forbes and Smart Money.

Lesson: #110. *Sometimes you can use the frequent flyer miles you accumulated to purchase money conscious magazines like Forbes and Fortune. Check with your airline for details.*

Since I began writing this book, the Stock Market has declined significantly but I still believe it will recover. When it does, the people who are buying stocks now will benefit the most.

STOP RENTING! PURCHASE A HOME

__Lesson: #111.__ You can save a bundle by bidding on homes at auctions and by buying foreclosed homes.

Wise up! You are never going to get ahead by handing over your paycheck to your landlord every month (and that's exactly what you are doing if you are renting). Even if you think that you're not ready to purchase a home, or you may not know where to begin, schedule an appointment with a realtor.   By doing so, you can get some pointers on improving your credit (if you need to), and information on down payment assistant programs. Realtors will point you in the right direction by telling you what steps you need to take or how much money is required down. That way, you'll at least have a GOAL in mind to work toward. Start going to open-house events and get familiar with the buying process, so that when you are financially ready, you'll know exactly what to do.

If you get quoted a higher mortgage than you expected, don't get discouraged. You can always rent out a couple of the rooms and divide it evenly just among the renters. When you are actually ready to buy a house, ask the real-estate agent to find a home with equity already in it. If a house is being sold for a great price but it's not necessarily in a town that you want to reside in, still consider buying it. You can rent it out and have the tenants pay off most of your mortgage and sell it for a profit later. Once you get approved for a mortgage, try to pay it off as soon as possible so you incur minimal interest. One method I read, is to pay an extra 10% on your mortgage each month and by the end of the year it will add up to be a whole extra payment.   One of the biggest, smartest, and most profitable investments you can make is purchasing a home.

GET AN EDUCATION

Lesson: #112. ***Society values college degrees. A degree does not necessarily prove that you are smart, but it does show that you are a persistent, reliable, and committed individual.***

Education is your leverage for getting what you want in most cases. When you have a good education you have more negotiating **power**. Whether the GOAL at hand is a promotion at your job, a new car, or money, the most educated gets the pick of the litter. If you don't have a high school diploma it's not too late, you can still get your GED. College isn't for everyone. If you happen to be one of those people, you can always learn a trade, which cuts your school time in half in most cases. If you are good at cosmetology, interior decorating, doing hair, or giving massages, then get licensed to do it so that you can start legally charging customers. If you have the intelligence and patience for college, I would suggest that you take the steps to enroll as soon as possible. The younger you are the easier it will be on you, because you may still remember some useful information from high school (like math formulas).

You can be successful without ever going to college. As a matter of fact, many of the world's most successful people don't have college degrees, but I'd suggest that you get a degree if you are able to… *because it's better to have it and not need it, than need it and not have it.* You may never have to use it but at the very least it's a good conversation starter. If you don't know what you want to major in, business is always a good choice. With the knowledge you gain you can start your own business or apply the info you learned to your everyday life.

When I was in college, I preferred to take most of my classes online, that way I was still able to travel as long as I had my laptop and wireless internet card. That may be an option that will work for you. You have to be a self-starter and make sure to turn in your assignments when they are due. You may be excited, but it's important to not overload your system. You don't have to enroll full time especially if you've been out of school for a while. Just take a class or two until you get into the swing of things. The summer sessions are a good way to double up on classes because you're able to take twice as many credits because the summer sessions are so short.

You can research grants and scholarships to assist you with tuition and fees if needed. Some sites include www.FASFA.ed.gov and www.Fastweb.com for financial assistance. You can also get information on grants and scholarships at your local library. You'd be surprised at the requirements for some scholarships funded by the government and many private organizations. I've come across scholarships for veterans, single mothers, Christians, and even to people with blue eyes. There are even scholarships for individuals and all you have to do is write an essay stating why you're in need of the money. You never know unless you try, so start putting those applications in. In many cases, you can use the money not only on tuition and fees but also on anything you desire, (like rent, food and clothes). Back in my college days, scholarships paid my rent many times.

OPEN YOUR OWN BUSINESS

This is the shortest secret to explain but don't underestimate it because it's one of the most important. Owning your own business is like a having a shield against Uncle Sam. It doesn't have to be a huge company either, in fact it can be a little business that you run on the internet. Having a registered corporation comes with many tax advantages; when it's time to do your taxes you can write off a lot of expenses such as eating out and traveling legally. Talk to a financial advisor about the legalities.

READ

Lesson: #113. *Books contain timeless knowledge. Go to the library or a bookstore and read a book that you wouldn't normally read. I challenge you to expand your horizons; I guarantee you will learn something new.*

Listed are some books that I've found useful when it came to conditioning my mind and enlightening me on matters of finance.

8 Reasons Why Successful People Derail, by L. Frankel

48 laws of Power, by Robert Greene

101 Mistakes Women Make that Sabotage their Careers, by Lois P. Frankel

A Beginner's Guide to Short Term Trading, by T. Turner

A Million Bucks by 30, by Alan Corey

Automatic Millionaire, by David Bach

Cracking the Millionaire Code, by Robert G. Allen

Eat That Frog, by Brian Tracy

Feel the Fear & Do It Anyway, by Susan Jeffers

Free Money for Everybody, by Matthew Lesko

Girl Get Your Money Straight, by Glinda Bridforth

Girl Make your Money Grow*,* by G. Bridgforth

Get Anyone to do Anything, by David J. Lieberman

Get in Touch with Your Inner Bitch, by Hilts

Get Rich, Stay Rich, Pass it on, by Catherine S. McBreen

Make Money Not Excuses, by Jean Chatzky

Memory Power, by Scott Hagwood

Never be Lied to Again, by David J. Lieberman

Nice Girls Don't Get Rich, by Lois P. Frankel

Retire Young Retire Rich, by Robert T. Kiyosaki

Rich Dad Poor Dad, by Robert T. Kiyosaki

Rich Woman, by Kim Kiyosaki

Save Smart Earn More, by Dennis Blitz

Secrets of the Millionaire Mind, by T. Harv Eker

The Art of Seduction, by Robert Greene

The Art of War, by Sun Tzu

The Idiot's Guide to Improving Your Credit Score,
by L. Epstein

The Idiot's Guide to Investing in Mutual Funds,
by Lita Epstein

The Idiot's Guide to Investing in Stocks, by R. Burgess

The Millionaire Next Door, by Thomas J. Stanley

The Power of Focus, by Les Hewitt

The Secret, by Rhonda Byrne

Think and Grow Rich, by Napoleon Hill

Who Took My Money? by Robert T. Kiyosaki

Who Moved My Cheese? by Spencer Johnson

Why Men Love Bitches, by Sherry Argov

Women & Money, by Suze Orman

Lesson: #114. ***INVESTING is a millionaire's secret to
success. That's how the rich get richer, so go to a library
and start reading.***

These books also reference other books, so you'll have
plenty of material to help you get ahead. One of the truest
statements I've heard is: the only thing that will impact your
life between now and next year is the people you meet and
the books you read. After you've completed my book, I urge
you to buy at least one of the books that I listed and add the
rest to your *Wish List.* Instead of getting a new pair of shoes,
get a book. You'll thank me later when you're able to use
the information that you gained to multiply your money.

If you'd like to get all the books listed but can't afford every book on the list, then form a book club among your girlfriends and keep rotating the books until you've read them all. You can also look online for sites that sell used books at a discounted price (like BetterWorldBooks.com and BookFinder.com). If you are on a super-tight budget then see if your local library has any of the books on the list. If all else fails, you can read them right in the bookstore.

One GOAL for most people is to own their **own home** free and clear. The sooner you stop renting, the sooner you can start owning, but of course that takes money. If you own your **own business** or have a good **education** the likelihood of you being able to make, understand, and manage money increases. Once you understand how money works, it will be easier to **budget, save,** and **invest** it. If you weren't educated on those subjects in school then you can teach them to yourself by **reading.** If you don't have enough cash, another alternative is to use your **credit**. It's imperative that you keep your credit score up to use that option. Unless you have a great deal of money stashed away, then it's a great idea to get **health, disability, and life insurance.** In the event that something happens to you before you reach your GOALs, your family and loved ones are taken care of.

SHARE WHAT YOU'VE GAINED

I bet you didn't see this one coming. I wouldn't go as far as saying that it's better to give than to receive, but giving to someone in need is definitely a great feeling. In the process of accomplishing your GOALs make sure that you give back to those less fortunate. Whether it's lending a hand, donating money or volunteering your time for a greater cause; there are so many people in the world that you can help in some way. You can deliver food to the elderly through Meals on Wheels, you can visit patients in the hospital, you can be a mentor to a child through the Boys & Girls Club, you can donate the clothes you don't wear anymore to the Salvation Army, you can feed the homeless through your church, or even teach adults to read through your local library branch. I'm sure there are things you'd like to change in your past, well…the bad news is that you still can't change it, but by sharing the mistakes you made and the lessons you learned you may be able to steer others in the right direction. I'm a firm believer that good deeds have a way of coming back to you.

Lesson: #115. Weed the dream killers from your life and shake the haters off.

I gave you a jumpstart and the blueprint on how to have a secure financial future. Now you have to do your part. You are near the end of the book but your journey starts here. Nothing I taught you will work, if you don't put your plan into action or if you're surrounded by negative influences and people that are working against you (weeds). It's time to do some gardening Honey, start plucking the weeds!

SECTION: VI

Who Is Baje?

Chapter 10

A DIAMOND IN THE ROUGH

...Before you judge me, get to know me.

A lump of coal is just that. It's only when extreme heat and pressure is applied, then intense polishing takes place, that a diamond surfaces.

A Diamond in the Rough

...In the Beginning

My earliest childhood memories are from when I was 5 years old, living on 1354 Pacific Street in Brooklyn, New York. I had an awesome day at school and couldn't wait to tell my parents how great it was. I arrived home excited; I opened the front door to our building and ran all the way up three flights of stairs. Out of breath, I pushed our heavy apartment door open. When I entered I saw my mother sitting in the middle of our family room all alone; my excitement instantly turned into confusion. She was sitting in an old white rocking chair that she had rocked me to sleep in many nights. She had light gray eyes that reminded me of the sky at times... today they were very cloudy, today they were raining. Tears slowly trickled down her cheeks and she had a look on her face that was totally foreign to me. It was a look of despair. She had always been a cheerful church going woman who would randomly burst into songs of praises.

As I looked around our home a sudden feeling of sadness set in. I was accustomed to coming home and hearing gospel songs blasting from the stereo speakers, but today it was quiet and it even had a lot more space. Most of the furniture was gone, even my father's big green suede couch. As young as I was, I knew that something was terribly wrong. I was just about to ask Mom about the furniture, when the most important question flooded my mind and overflowed through my lips. Immediately I asked where my father was. In a despondent tone, she responded,

"He doesn't live here anymore."

I thought that surely there must be some mistake because my daddy loved me and he told me so all the time. My daddy would never leave me. I began asking my mother a great deal of questions. *Why did he leave? Was it something I did? How come he didn't tell me goodbye? Did you tell him to leave us? Where did he go? Is he ever coming back?* But my questions were left unanswered. She just looked at me, and then looked past me as if I wasn't even there.

Two years old.

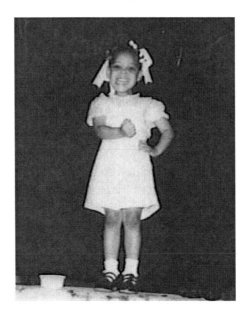

Five years old.

Just when I was getting accustomed to my mom being the only parent at home, my fragile life was hit with another whirlwind. Soon after my parents' separation, with haste I was shipped to Jamaica to live with my aunt Willet and grandmother Syble. Jamaica was my home for the next eight years.

Even though my parent's marriage didn't work out, my father remained in close contact with me. He supported me financially and made sure that I received all the necessary essentials and went to one of the most prestigious schools in Jamaica (St. Hilda's High). My father decided that going to school in Jamaica was the best thing for me, because the education system was safer and so much more advanced. Brooklyn was a terrible place to raise a child because of the crime and teenage pregnancy rate. He wanted me to be more than another statistic. Just a few months later his decision to re-locate me was validated, because my brother Tone (who also lived with us) was shot in the head twice. He was only fifteen years old at the time.

I was raised in a small town in Jamaica called Mile End, as the name implies that's what this place was for most people. Most people never got the chance to see another side of life; they lived there, went to school there, got married there and died there. Since the age of six, whenever a teacher would ask me what I wanted to be when I grew up, I would always say:

"I want to be a model".

My classmates would burst into laughter telling me that it would never happen. I couldn't blame them because they didn't know any better. Hardly anyone ever escaped Mile End. Mile End has a way of demolishing hopes and dreams as quickly as they are constructed, but I believe that *anyone without hopes and dreams ceases to exist*. I was kind of tomboyish, so all they saw was my rugged exterior: my skinny legs, big feet and short nappy hair. I used to climb trees and run around barefoot. They couldn't see my vision or know what was in my heart, but that didn't keep me from dreaming and believing. I've always been a dreamer. In between classes I was always writing about the things that I wanted to have and the places that I saw on TV that I wanted to visit.

My grandmother was the first person to put the idea of modeling in my head. When I complained to her about being skinny, having a flat chest, and how my collar bones protruded, she'd tell me that all the supermodels in the magazines and on TV looked like me and they weren't only gorgeous but were also making big bucks. I believed her. My grandmother began making clothes for me and started signing me up for neighborhood fashion shows. The clothes she made were by no means couture. The styles were a bit outdated and a few sizes too big, but when I wore them I felt like I belonged on a runway. She introduced me to the world of fame and fashion and my appetite grew and it never stopped growing since then.

I remember our house in Jamaica vividly. It was small, painted gray and white, and had a rusty brown zinc roof that leaked. At the first smell of rain we had to place buckets all over the house to catch the water that leaked from the roof. I remember laying in bed many times just watching the water beads roll off the ceiling and into the buckets. To me, it was a normal part of life. *I can still hear the rhythm of the rain-drops.* During hurricane season we'd have to tie the roof down with rope and put twenty-pound cement blocks on it to keep the roof from blowing off. One time we didn't tie it down correctly and a hurricane blew the roof off the house completely! We didn't have hot water or a kitchen sink for that matter. We had to catch water outside in pans just to wash the dishes. A lot of people lived in this small community and the water supply wasn't always enough for our entire neighborhood. Sometimes we'd have to walk over the hills to the next community and bring water back in buckets on our heads. *You can only imagine what that did to our hair-styles.* We had to wash our clothes by hand and hang them in the backyard on the clotheslines to dry. Nine of us lived in that tiny house but we had many fun-filled days- they were beautiful days, wonderful days. We learned to laugh despite living in poverty. It was hard, but struggling in Mile End was far better than the high possibility of ending up dead in Brooklyn.

By the age of fourteen, I managed to make it out of Mile End and still dodge Brooklyn by moving to Florida with my mother. I had big dreams; I wanted nothing more than to be on my own, to prove to my family and peers that I was going somewhere in life and that I was going to be *somebody*. No matter how hard I tried...*life* got in the way.

Upon my return from Jamaica, I learned that my mother still hadn't fully recovered from my father leaving her. She was diagnosed with clinical depression some years prior as a result. She would be fine at times and then when she didn't take her medicine she'd slip into an emotionless state. Those were the most difficult times because she wouldn't eat anything, talk to anyone, or even get a good night's sleep. From the room next door I would hear her sobbing, but I'd feel useless because there was nothing I could possibly do to ease her pain. She just sat there and looked at me, and then looked past me, as if I was five years old all over again. That emotionless stare held me captive. No matter how many years passed, when that gaze resurfaced, I re-played the first day I saw it and re-lived the emptiness I felt at that moment – because whether I wanted to or not I felt her pain. *That vacant feeling remained embedded in my chest, and served as a piercing reminder to never give a guy that much of my heart, that if he left I would be devastated.*

After living with my mother for only one month, the State declared my mother an unfit parent because of her depression and placed me in foster care. At the age of fifteen I tried to get emancipated so I could work and live on my own legally. I told the judge that I was fully capable of taking care of myself. Reluctantly, he denied my request and reiterated that even though I was mature for my age, I was still too young. Maybe the fact that I wore my hair in a ponytail, had on some pedal pushers, didn't have a job and didn't even graduate from high school may have weighed on his decision to rule unfavorably. He gave me a checklist of things that I had to complete:

> I had to produce a detailed plan on how I was going to support myself.
> I could not get arrested or get in trouble with the law.
> I had to be employed and keep the job for more than six months.
> I had to get my high school diploma.
> I had to complete their independent living classes.
> I had to have at least three thousand dollars saved in the bank in case of an unforeseen emergency.

After I completed everything I'd be able to petition again. He wished me luck and sent me on my way.

Fifteen years old.

Living in foster care wasn't easy. I went through eighteen homes in the span of two years. There were times I was tired of trying and many times I wanted to give up and stop working so hard but I didn't. Less than two years later I completed everything on that checklist...as a bonus, I even got my driver's license. I didn't know when or even how I was going to buy a car, but I got my license just in case I was able to afford one somewhere down the road. Right before I turned seventeen years old, I enrolled in college and the judge granted my request to be emancipated. I was thrilled, because I was now legally an adult, accountable for my actions and able to make my own decisions. Within those two years while I worked on the checklist, I even bought kitchen utensils, decorations for a home, and pieces of furniture bit by bit. My friends laughed at me, saying that it was stupid of me to waste my money buying all those items and I didn't even have an apartment but I didn't let their opinions deter me from my GOAL. As soon as I got emancipated, the first thing I did was get my own place and another job to help pay for my college classes. To their surprise, I had absolutely everything I needed the first day that I moved in. *They couldn't see my vision, they said I was pushing my cart before my horse...but that tactic always worked for me.*

At the age of seventeen, my body began to develop and take on the form of a woman. It was clear that my transition from adolescence to womanhood wasn't going to be an easy one. *I had more to worry about than just surviving and making ends meet, now I had to deal with bigger problems...men.*

...When I was a child, I spoke as a child, but now that I am a woman, I speak my mind.

Throughout my life, I've had conflicts with males. Many of whom would only offer their assistance at a cost. They'd only work with me if I stroked their ego, suppressed my confident attitude, or became their concubine or woman. A few even bluntly demanded that I'd have to have sex with them. Thank God I didn't fall for that. *Being strong-willed was never a choice; it's just the way I had to be to survive.* I made the decision to never allow anyone to make me feel ashamed. If I ever made the decision to give myself to a man, it would be because I wanted to. If it were for any other reason, then that meant I would not be the one holding the cards and I would give up control. *What is between my legs is mine and I'm not going to give it up because an ego-driven guy thinks that his money or authority gives him the license to possess me.*

Prime example: my childhood dream was to be a model, so once I legally became an adult I pursued it. On my eighteenth birthday I took up the Orlando yellow pages and began calling modeling agencies in my area. All of them said that I needed professional photos if I wanted to book paid jobs. I was a college student working two jobs and all the money that I earned was going towards my bills. I wanted to have the right tools for my craft but I just couldn't afford them. I told a good friend of mine named Rob about my dilemma. He said that he heard about a photographer in our area that did very good work, *let's call him Sherman Sheffield.* Rob then said that he would schedule a shoot for me and take care of the cost even thought it was $500 because he knew just how much it meant to me. He kept his word and a week later I shot with *Sherman.* Rob even accompanied me on the shoot to assure that all went well. Everything went smoothly and I was very happy with my photos.

A few weeks later *Sherman* called me to schedule another shoot for the following day. I really wanted to shoot again but I declined because I didn't have it within my budget to spend $500 on photos. He said that he was so impressed with my posing and professionalism that he wasn't going to charge me for this shoot because he knew that we could make money together in the future. I was thrilled and thanked him from the bottom of my heart. Once I hung up the phone I hurried to the mall before closing time and bought a few things to shoot in. When I got back home I tried on quite a few outfits and practiced my poses in the full-length mirror in my bedroom. A few hours later I went to bed and had pleasant dreams about the upcoming shoot. *Sherman* seemed like a nice guy with good intentions. I had no indications that things would go wrong based on my first shoot with him, so this time I made the decision to go by myself. It was a long, but exciting shoot. We shot on the beach, in an alley on the highway and even in an abandoned building; the shoot started at sunrise and ended at sundown.

Throughout the day *Sherman* told me to relax and assured me that he wasn't the least bit interested in me sexually. He said that the only thing he was interested in was producing the best quality photos so that we both could make money off of them. As the day progressed I let down my guard because I had no reason to doubt what he was saying. At the end of the shoot, when it was time for me to get my photos, I was shocked out of my mind when *Sherman* started telling me how sexy I was and how much he wanted me. I was barely legal! I had just turned eighteen a few days prior. When I shut down his advances he told me that if I didn't have sex with him then he wasn't going to give me my photos. *I couldn't believe what I was hearing. I spent all day in the sun taking the pictures, how could he do this to me?* As bad as I wanted the photos and even though they could have helped me with my career I didn't give in to his absurd demands. When I thought he wasn't looking I took some of the photos and then I told him that I was ready to go home, so he gave me a ride back.

Thirty minutes later we were seated in his car and about half way to my house when he told me that he knew that I had some of the photos and he wasn't going to take me home until I gave them back. We argued for about two minutes and I kept stressing that it was not fair or rational for him to act that way, but he didn't care. He made a U-turn and entered Interstate 4, which was the opposite direction from where I lived. Now I was nervous. I dug in my purse and took out my phone. I was trying to stay calm, but my body began giving in to my state of mind. My hands were shaking and my heart was beginning to pound louder and faster. I called Rob and explained to him what was taking place, I thought I would get some reassurance when he picked up, but I just got more nervous when I heard the fear in his voice. He wanted to come and get me right away, but I was in a car on a freeway going 70 miles per hour. With each second that passed I was getting further and further away from the last exit number I told Rob that I was at. I took a few deep breaths to try and slow down the pace of my heart beat so I could stop being scared and try to think things through. Many thoughts raced through my head. I knew I only had a few moments to make a decision because if I waited until he was at his destination to try to get out then I would be on his territory. I had to think quickly. He started exiting off the freeway, and right off the exit he caught a red light. As the car rolled up to the light I knew this was my best chance to escape. I had two big bags and a purse with me. Quickly I threw my bags out the window, pushed the door open and jumped out of the rolling vehicle. I was almost out of the car when he snatched my purse with all my money, debit cards and identification in it. He accelerated and sped off into the distance.

I walked to the nearest hotel, called Rob and waited in the lobby until he arrived. Within fifteen minutes he came to my rescue. I called *Sherman* and told him that he could have the pictures back and all I wanted was my purse. He told me that he was going to call the police if I contacted him again and I'd go to jail for stealing. The thought of going to jail scared me so much that I never did call him again. I didn't realize that I was the *victim* and he would have been the one to go to jail for kidnapping.

Another example, I was about nineteen years old when I flew to New Jersey from Florida by myself for a modeling competition. A national black men's magazine had a strong presence there and I ended up landing a shoot with them. Finally, I felt like I was getting closer to my dream and I was ecstatic. I told all my friends about the shoot and they all were just as excited as I was. Weeks following the shoot I kept in contact with the editor to find out when my layout would hit stands. *Let's call him Marcus.* Marcus would always tell me "next issue" and then quickly change the subject by asking when we were going to hang out and have dinner. I lightly brushed him off each time. I remember our last phone conversation vividly. When he started getting personal, I flat out told him that I wasn't interested in dating him and I just wanted to know the publication date of the issue that I'd be in. He said that I wasn't going to be in it anymore because I stood him up. I couldn't believe my ears and I honestly thought that he was joking, so I asked:

"Are you saying that I can't get in your magazine because I won't go out with you?"

He responded,

"Yes."

He said that it was much bigger than him because he knew all the players in the industry that could make me a "star". He told me that he was spoiled and now I know what I needed to do... *whatever that meant.*

Looking back, I'm glad that I experienced those mishaps when I was a clueless teen just trying to make it, because I view them only as learning experiences that have made me wiser. If any guy came at me that way now, with no doubt in my mind, he'd be dealt with accordingly. Needless to say, I never did get the rest of my pictures from Sherman and I didn't grace the pages of Marcus' magazine because there was no way I was going to spread my legs, or even sit through dinner with guys whose behavior absolutely repulsed me. It's their loss, because since then I've worked with a dozen reputable publications. They probably wouldn't know what a woman smelled like if they weren't in the industry. There are many guys who prey on young and naïve girls with big dreams. Guys like them have motivated me to write this book, so that other females will avoid similar situations.

I've been a victim many times, but one day I reached a cross road. I made a decision to decide. I was no longer just going to go along with the flow and allow people and situations to dictate my life. It was time to do some soul searching. Every time life pushed me down, I could stay down and cry and wait for someone to save me or I could jump back up, learn from what happened, and make sure it didn't happen again. I decided that I went through too much in my life to get distracted, I beat too many odds to fail now.

I made GOALs, I made a plan, I surrounded myself with positive people and I stayed focused. I was determined to meet all my GOALs and I wasn't going to fall victim to game. I refused to be a victim.

Your life will change when you decide that you will no longer be the victim.

Years ago I came across a quote that kept me strong. I love it so much that I'd like to share it with you. "Life kicks you around sometimes, it scares you and it beats you up, but there's one day when you realize you're not just a survivor, you are a fighter. You're tougher than anything life throws your way."

...The Conclusion

Lesson: #116. ***The only one that will never let you down is you.***

Consciously I jumped off the defense and I was now on the offense...and I was winning. I was winning because now I decided the *plays* in the *playbook*. I was no longer an adolescence trying to find my way and afraid of getting hurt. I was no longer a *lady* who only spoke when spoken to. I realized that it was up to me to protect myself by shielding my mind and my heart. I became a *woman* when I realized that I had the **power**. I had the **power** to pick, choose, and refuse. I had a voice, I had standards, and I also had limits. Now I was the one who decided who I allowed in my life, how close they got to me, in what manner they spoke to me, and how much I would accept from them. I transformed into a *woman* who knew what she wanted and wasn't going to stop until she got it. Gaining momentum, I was no longer afraid to push aside or utilize any obstacles who tried to stop me from accomplishing my GOALs.

You have the **Power**, Use It! You are beautiful, talented, and strong. You can do *anything* you put your mind to; you just have to stop doubting yourself. We as women have to stick together. Let's stop putting the next sister down and try to lift her up instead. I urge you to pass the *shovel* (useful knowledge you've learned) along to another woman who needs a little guidance because it may save her life. Life is so much bigger than you and it's so much bigger than me. It's about living, learning, and teaching others what we've learned. Some people have children, some people plant trees...this is one of my ways of leaving a legacy. Sharing my experiences by writing this book so other women will not be taken advantage of was one of my life GOALs. I gave you enough information so you're able to not only recognize opportunities when they come along, but also heed warning signs.

...To the Critics

I was born the 7th day of March in the year 1984. Long before that, there were movies, articles and books written about how to be a player. In fact, in 1997 a film called "How to be a Player" was viewed by millions. It was a comedy about a playboy with only one goal in life: to have sex with as many women as possible. I would've found it hilarious if that wasn't the goal of so many men in real life.

With the boom of the internet, men have been getting even savvier. I even met a man who wrote a book called Copy, Paste, Bang (How to meet women on the internet and have sex with them)??! So you see... I'm just making the best of what I am given to work with. One critic went as far as saying that I'm taking advantage of men. Well let me say that I'm not stealing, making false promises, giving them drugs or my body, and all the men who gave me money or gifts gave willingly; I didn't threaten them or twist their arms.

Most guys think with their heads (and not the one on their shoulders). When they see a woman, they don't wonder what type of person she is. They don't care about her GOALs and aspirations in life or how they can aid her to achieve her vision. When they see a woman the first thought that runs through their minds is: how can I get with that? It's like an unwritten law of nature that most guys want sex from women - whether it's a one-night-stand or the "in-home" kind, (the majority of them lean towards the first of the two). I can't stop men from approaching me; I can't stop men from being men. The best that I can do is position myself in the types of settings where they're of a better grade. I didn't create the game but I've come to terms that it does exist; so I'm forced to play it calculated, trying to survive like the rest of the world.

So many women give in to men that mean them no good, and as a result are forced to give up on their dreams. They end up having babies while they're children themselves, they end up having abortions that they spend their whole lives regretting. They end up dropping out of school; some look in the mirror and are unable to recognize who they've become, all because they've settled. They didn't know about the wonderful things that the world has to offer and the treasures left to be explored. They didn't know about the opportunities that are available if only they had the courage to venture out. They didn't have someone in their lives to motivate them, to teach them, to push them, and to tell them what to steer clear of.

At the end of the day if my views, my experiences, my advice or my book helps one person then I am fulfilling my purpose in life. If you don't agree with my views then don't buy the book. Leave it on the shelf so that a woman who really needs it can learn some things. There's a woman out there who just lost everything, there's a woman that's heard she'll never amount to anything, there's a woman that's not in the "in crowd," there's a woman who has lost someone she loved, there's a woman who is making tremendous sacrifices now because she can see the bigger picture. There is a woman who wants a better life but doesn't know where to start. This book serves as motivation for all those women, because at one point or another I was each of those women.

It hurts me when I see a girl so drunk that she has to be put in a taxi by strangers. It makes me sad when women are at the mercy of men because they don't have an education or a good career. It's very disturbing to hear stories about the sex acts that some women have taken part in just so they can get some money to buy food for their children. It brought tears to my eyes when I watched a video on YouTube where a guy bragged about how he knowingly gave one hundred women the HIV virus and how easy it was to lure them in bed because he drove a Mercedes Benz. *As if that wasn't bad enough, he listed all their names also.* I'm not telling women to live a lifestyle which they don't approve of, what I am saying is that if a woman is already living a similar lifestyle, then this is a faster, safer way to do it…because frankly, I've heard enough sad stories.

Did you ever notice that most of the people that are constantly putting you down and telling you that you are doing things the wrong way aren't the same people you can go to when you need help? Exactly! So let them talk, chances are they'll have something negative to say regardless of what you do; like the words to Mary J. Blige song states: "They'll never be happy because they're not happy with themselves"

Don't Hate the Digger… Grab the Gold!

FORGET EVERY THING I SAID!

When it's Not "Mr. Right Now,"
And it's Actually "Mr. Right."

Forget Everything I Said!

My friend Mike said:

"Baje, at some point most women will probably give it up."

I told him:

"I agree, but it should not be for money or money alone. Sex is a wonderful thing when it's someone who worked for you and who deserves you. After all, we are human with sexual needs and fantasies to be fulfilled."

There are good men out there, *even though they may be as rare as a sighting of Big Foot.* If and when you do find one, and you want to keep him, then none of these rules apply. Detoxify your mind and erase everything you've read from your head because there are whole set of guidelines to go by to treat and serve a man who actually deserves you. When you find one that earns your respect, devotion, love, and body you have to treasure him because they don't come around often. Hopefully, you know the difference between "The One" and the fools out there that use, abuse and mistreat women.

If you ever find "The One", remember that men are accustomed to being the aggressors, so you'll have to throw him a curve ball and take control of your sex-life occasionally. Be creative, be his escape from reality. Have him anxious to come home from a long day's work. There is nothing like new booty to a man, so behind closed doors *let your hair down and become the other woman* and cheating will never cross his mind. You have to tune into him, build trust and ask him about his fantasies so you both can live them out together. The only way he won't get bored is when you both connect mentally and you understand what he wants so you can give it to him in ways that no other woman has. You have to match your sexual appetite to his. You have to be unselfish, be willing to try new things, and make a conscious effort to spice things up. Once you find out what he likes, you have to perfect it, and never let the passion or intensity diminish.

In my next book I'll share with you some intense, explicit and seductive stories. Whether you want to read them to get your juices flowing, or whisper the naughty parts in his ear right before you devour him, these stories will certainly get you both in an erotic frame of mind.

LOOK OUT FOR MY NEXT BOOK

Aphrodisiac

Bonus Inserts

TESTIMONIALS & LETTERS

...From Friends, and Fans.

Testimonials & Letters

I met Baje just over two years ago and have been amazed by her focus, determination, and compassion towards success. From modeling to acting, Baje is a natural. She began her career with the philosophy that you get out of life what you put into it. What started out as a simple dream has propelled into reality. Baje also recently embarked on her newest venture of book writing. I'm sure this will only serve as the beginning of a long lustrous journey that ends up in the parking lot of success. With her radiant beauty, talent, charisma, and brains, the sky is the limit for this entrepreneur. So be advised: this woman knows what she wants and won't stop until she gets it.

- Anthony Truss
Operation co-coordinator of Sony Music Entertainment

There are many imitators, there are many haters, and there are many lovers of the one and only Baje. We first met at my first fashion show in 2002 she was one of my models ...There is a lot of competition out there and people can be cruel, it takes a lot of courage to do what Baje has done. Baje does things HER way and she will run over you if you get in the way of where she is going. I'm still trying to figure out if she runs on batteries. I wish I could live so freely as she does, I wouldn't be able to survive in my world without three jobs. I never understood how Baje could be so serious and not be at all flirtatious and still get these guys to give her money. Guys are seriously weak for Baje. She knows the game and I'm learning from her...she has the looks, charisma, style, and attitude. When she gets thousands of dollars

she upgrades what she has and moves on. I think that there should be a school that teaches young women to take tax-free money from rich men and invest it into whatever they want and make it grow! (Hint, hint)

Baje I think by teaching women about investing and encouraging them to purchase homes. In your own way you are helping to rebuild the economy. I think you need to go to Capitol Hill and visit the politicians and see how many of our tax dollars you can get back LOL. I'm Proud of you. Thanks for all the times you were there for me, our friendship has passed the test...we will take the world by storm each in our own way; we will survive and get what we want. Love Ya!

-BFF Chelle Chell

Baje is a party girl but a go-getter who will do whatever it takes to make it. She loves the finer things in life and loves to travel; she's fun to be around. When she walks in a room, she lights it up! She is a wonderful friend to me and will bend over backwards for her friends.

- Joanna

Hello Baje, I just wanted to take a moment to compliment you on your work. I take no shame in giving credit where it's due and you definitely deserve it. You have proven to be a true Go-Getter. You set the bar high for other models to follow. Congratulations on all your success.

- Camille from Myspace

Before I met, Baje I realized that I didn't know what it was like to be a BITCH LOL (I really don't use that word but whatever). I respect her for a lot of reasons, one of which is we share a similar zeal for going after our dreams and turning them into GOALs and not giving up no matter what obstacles and speed bumps may occur. It's all about prepping for the payoff! Her personality helped me learn how to stand up for myself more. *Big up ya self chick, keeping on keeping it haute.*

- Lisa Leggz (Partner Lease A Star, llc.)

Wow! LA huh? Congrats and I wish you the best blessings ever. Sorry we never really got to get too much acquainted. I really admire you as a person because you inspire me to go after things I really would like to conquer. So much love on that. Hopefully, we can link up one day...
- Donesha (Glitz &Glamour Model)

I met this young lady three years ago when I was in Orlando Florida. At the time I was with my clients Hoopz and Lyric. We had breakfast, and she explained to me what she wanted to do in the business. I find Baje to be one of a kind woman. She is very stern on what she wants to do plus she knows how she should look from head to toe. I find her to be a loyal person period, and someone everyone should get to know. I am very happy that we got to work together to shoot for my magazine TitaniumGirlz, and we will continue to work together.

-Van Silk CEO/Publisher TITANIUMGIRLZ, & Magazine

I'm just writing to let you know that your accomplishments are amazing...I think when we first added each other I was in Gainesville, and you were in Orlando...well you sure got yourself in the scene...congrats!

-One black woman to another (Myspace)

Two words 'Hustler Couture'. You hustle like a man but you are feminine.

- Simone Mighty (friend)

Ambitious! That is you all the way!

-Tsick (Member of Rap group TREAL)

Just a quick little note to say hi and to tell you that I'm so proud of you! Congrats on all your recent achievements, you've always been such a positive inspiration. XOXOXO

- Jess (Glitz & Glamour Model)

Women like you are the reason for this calendar. There are so many young women throwing their lives away, and they feel like they can't do better for themselves. I think that it would be an inspiration to any young lady to meet someone like you, just to be able to say, "She's from the same city as I am, and she's doing it! Why can't I?" So in all your efforts to make your dreams come true, always

remember that you may be someone's role model or their inspiration, always carry yourself with that in mind. God bless.

- Most Beautiful & Driven Women of 2008 Calendar

I just want to say you look great! I am very proud of you for pursuing your dream and succeeding! Kisses ~ p.s. I miss the Jus Modelz meetings!

-La Kendra
(Member of my organization for women 'Jus Modelz')

Baje is a fun woman to be around...unpredictable and open-minded. She is very driven, and business minded. You find few females like her and that's what made me like her more as a friend. She's destined to be very successful.

- Nasheeka (Friend)

It's been over two years since we've spoken, we were very good friends and one bad situation broke us apart, I really loved you. You use to inspire and motivate me and it seems like ever since we stopped being friends my life shifted to the left. I now have two kids, a girl (almost two years old) and a boy (seven months)! I have been trying to get back in shape, being an accomplished model was always a dream of mine because so many people doubted me...and they still do! I just want to know if you can forgive and forget and maybe help me get back in the game. I just want to know if you are willing to motivate me like you use to. I still love you and miss you and congratulations on your success!

- (X Friend)

Thoughts on the Dr. "Dill" Show

A few months ago, I was a guest on an international television talk show to debate the topic: Gold Diggers. *For legal purposes, let's call it the Dr. "Dill" Show.* Even before meeting me, the host and producers already knew how they wanted to portray me. They didn't care about my story, my views or the real message I was conveying to women (Which is: *you don't have to settle, you don't have to use your body to get what you want, if you use your mind*). All they cared about was ratings, they even had a decoy.

The decoy went undercover as a limousine driver, but he was really an NFL player worth 76 million dollars. When the limousine arrived to pick me up, immediately, my sixth sense kicked in because there were two drivers. The camera lady quickly told me not to pay attention to the second person in the driver uniform because he was a "driver-in-training". Something seemed fishy about the whole situation because one driver (the one that was actually driving) remained silent the whole time. The other driver, (that was in the passenger seat), was constantly asking me questions. He even asked me if he could take me out on a date that night. That's when I knew for sure that he was working undercover. *Any person with any kind of sense wouldn't risk their job to flirt with a guest and go against protocol knowing that they were being filmed.* Usually I put guys through a screening process but because I knew that he was a decoy I told him that it was OK for us to go on a friendly date. *Come on now...I watch Maury and the Montel William show...I know how talk shows work.*

When we got to our destination I wanted him to know that I caught on to his game and I was a step ahead of him. So when I hopped out of the car I smiled at him, waved and said,

"Bye, Decoy."

He laughed because it was clearly evident that I knew his position. So, you can only imagine how shocked I was when I saw the final edited version of the episode and the producers cut the whole part out when I said that I knew the driver was a decoy. *Now the whole world was going to think that they actually fooled me!* That night I could hardly sleep because I had so many thoughts running through my mind. It wasn't until I went on the show's website and read some of the comments that the viewers made, that I felt at ease.

The entertainment world is twisted and filled with illusion. You can't believe all you see or hear. They tried to mold me into the image that they wanted the world to see, but they didn't succeed.

Here are some of the comments that the viewers made...

The woman on today's show isn't doing anything that men don't do. Even though I've never by any means been a wealthy woman, I was able to take care of myself in my 20's. I've met more than my share of gold digging guys, only they want the sex too. They want sex & money. Love & respect are last on their list. That's the way men are and that will never change. I say if you can do it, TAKE 'EM! And take one for me! Settling down isn't for everyone!

Men are allowed to take what they want from women and then leave them, but women can't... why not???? If men want to give money or stuff, and they don't even know the girl well it's obvious that they only want sex....

Though gold digging might make a woman look self centered and lazy, I believe it is an art. Ups to Baje for getting men to do all those things for her without sleeping with them because many girls like me can't do it. A man who buys expensive jewelry for a woman he barely knows must have only one thing in mind - sex. Who has ever brought men on a show for using women for sex??

-Kisio123

Love lasts a few months or a few years and then the relationship is boring and old. Hot sex goes to no sex. Dates become sitting in front of the TV. Without money, you have to live in the same place all the time and can't even take vacations. I've been poor and I've been rich and life is a lot better with money!

If I could go back in time, I'd be a gold digger, but unfortunately, I didn't know what the world had to offer. If you marry [and the guy has money], you'll probably at least like the spouse as a friend when the passion dies. You'll have several houses so each of you can live the life you want. Everyone who

A Gold Digger's Guide

said that they want love instead of money or sex isn't willing to recognize that the divorce rate is 50% and most marriages really SUCK.

-Hound Heaven4

If the talk show host was a single woman trying to date men these days and find a loving relationship, he'd understand that unfortunately, no matter how good we are towards men, and how long we hold on and keep giving believing that men will finally appreciate us and give something back, the reality is that they never will.

I'm so glad the young lady [Baje] figured out the truth about men as early on as she did. Good for her.

-From an attractive woman, age 47, who finally realized the truth around age 46.

When I was naive about men, I would have been appalled by "gold diggers". Now, at age 47, I say, "You go Girl!" As a divorced mother of 2 daughters, I raised my children with no help of any sort from a man. I searched for many years for a "good" man believing the myth that one would show up, love us, and offer help. I had a few long-term relationships, and gave each of them everything I had, including money, to help the relationship function well. I received nothing back

except more responsibilities. The young
lady on your Gold Digger show [Baje]
fortunately accepted the reality that we
women are dealing with men as best we
can. It's not the Gold Diggers that you
need to work on. It's the 36%, (more
than $1/3^{rd}$), of the male population, who
simply want sex and have no interest in
the work of a relationship.

-A Moral Woman, Julie Fox

I find it disgusting that only women were
brought on as "gold diggers" and only men
were brought on as examples of success.
What kind of outrageous stereotypes are
you trying to perpetuate? Ever heard of a
sugar mama? Furthermore, what did these
men have to sell to get their money?
Unless they were born rich, they probably
had to sell their time, energy, and
dignity at least as much as a "gold
digger" would. How many of us have been
virtual slaves to a boss? These women are
entrepreneurs, they should be commended.
Obviously Baje is smart and successful on
her own terms - she just got some amazing
press and will now sell many more copies
of her book, and all she had to do was
place herself in a controversial
situation on television... Writing books
and allowing people to air dirty laundry
on TV in order to sell those books...
reminds me of a certain talk show
host/doctor that we know, and yet Baje
was told that she should be ashamed that
she isn't earning her own!? The other
obvious point is that these women are

being told that they might miss out on a good man if they only look at money. What kind of man looks at ugly fat women instead of hot women for fear that he might "miss a nice girl." Give me a break.

-Carava

Okay, Doc, you are an exceptional guy. You have never said to a woman, "It's a good thing I am a leg man, or I wouldn't have bought you a drink", or "I don't want to deal with your baggage, I just want to party with you." You have never said to your buddies "I'll take the blonde, you can have the pig", or "Who cares if she's (ditsy, loud, weepy, drunk, etc.) it's not like I'm going to marry her"? I could go on for pages on what men say to women, and to each other about women that is objectifying, demeaning, and dehumanizing.

How we are talked about shows the mindset, that we are property, and a commodity. Take, for instance, these common phrases, and how they can be applied, among men, with equal definition to a car, a house, and a woman: you need to get a___, that ___ is high maintenance, my life would be so much better if I had a new ____, you need to get rid of that old ____before it starts falling apart, etc..

I am sure that the world would be a wonderful place if a woman's worth were not based on superficial characteristics, and somewhere on any man's top three reasons to talk to a woman, AND on his list of what he wants in a mate (okay, number one) is that he found her beautiful, and who she really is came in a distant fourth after feeding him, and other slave labor. We spend a lot of time and money trying to be the premium model of the commodity; the blondest, biggest busted (while otherwise smallest), bluest eyed, and the least likely to express any needs of their own.

The point being, how can you demonize young women who are not valued for anything else, because they make the best that they can of the circumstances into which they were born?

-Lily

What about the men who use these women for their bodies and lie to them, and trick them into believing that they care about them? What about women feelings? I really applaud Baje. (Please don't let anyone discourage you from what you're doing. WOMAN TO WOMAN, I AM VERY PROUD OF YOU AND WHAT YOU'RE DOING).

-Love Lyshon

So those letters go to show that you can fool some of the people some of the time, but you can't fool all of the people all of the time.

A Gold Digger's Guide

Dear Mom

My mother survived breast cancer before I was born, but this time around the disease got the best of her. By the time she built up enough courage to accept and face the devastating diagnosis for the second time, the cancer had already spread to her lungs. It was too late for radiation treatment to work and six months later she lost the fight. I was nineteen years old at the time. My mom was a humble woman, she lived a very simple life and when she passed away she didn't have much. She had very little education so she wasn't able to secure a good-paying job. She never made it to high school and wasn't able to teach any of her children how pertinent education was. She didn't have a financial advisor to teach her about saving, budgeting, or investing. She didn't have a mentor or role model to let her know how essential having medical, life, and disability insurance were. My mother was a good woman. She had a pure heart and was always willing to lend a helping hand to people less fortunate. I wish she had someone to help guide her in some aspects of her life the way that I'm trying to guide other women now.

It's been six years since you passed away and I still can't grasp the concept that I will never ever see you again. It's just not fair. There's so much I want to ask you about men, motherhood, and life in general. There are so many places I want to take you to, there are so many things that I want to share with you. I've made new friends that I want you to meet. Just when I was getting to know you again...you left.

Prior to your departure you told me that

the doctors said the cancer was winning but you had a couple years to live and a couple months at worst; but only two weeks after that you were gone; gone forever. I didn't have enough time to prepare myself for the life-altering experience. Can anyone truly prepare for death? I know it wasn't your choice to go, but that doesn't ease the pain. There's so much you didn't experience, not because you didn't want to but because you just didn't know how much the world had to offer. People say: "**you only live once**" but most will never get the true essence of it until it hits too close to home.

As a child, I used to wonder where I got my looks from. Was it you or dad or a combination of both? With each year that passes, the answer becomes more evident. When I look in the mirror while getting ready for my daily errands...I see the striking resemblance. The almond shape of my eyes, the profile of my nose, and the outline of my lips...I look like you Mom. As a child I was perplexed about being sent to Jamaica. I couldn't understand how a mother could just send her six-year old girl away. Now that I'm a woman I know that it must have been hard for you, it was probably harder on you than it was on me. After all, you carried me for nine months, you watched your belly grow, and you nursed me. I realize now that *when you love someone you do what's best for them, even if it means letting them go.*

You lived your life and you did the best you could do for me and now it's time for me to live. Since you've been gone, I've accomplished some things that you never would have imagined. I know that this is only the beginning of my adventurous journey because I'm dedicated to experiencing all that life has to offer. In memory of you, I'll share with women each lesson I learned along the way, (I shared 116 lessons so far). I'm going to live life to the fullest and live a little extra for you too. I Love You.

- **Your last child of 10.**

Life
is a test; the score
is given by you.
What's wrong to another may be
right to you.
You can make mistakes, as long as you learn
The lesson from the previous page that you
turned,

What matters the most, is the effort you made
And the wisdom you pass, before it all fades.
There are two types of people, one hasn't a
clue:
Go-Getters and No-Getters…which one
are you?

-Baje

If you bought my book too late and already broke all the
rules, all is not lost. It's never too late for a new beginning.
Consider today the first day of your new life. *Enjoy* ☺.

JOIN THE MOVEMENT

AGoldDiggersGuide.com

BajeOnline.com

Twitter.com/ModelBaje

Myspace.com/ModelBaje

Myspace.com/GoalDiggersClub

Facebook.com/BajeFletcher

Youtube.com/HeyThereBuddyBJ

ILoveBaje@gmail.com

Baje is a life coach and available for public speaking engagements and one-on-one mentoring (in person, online and via phone). To schedule a session, or obtain more information on the GOAL DIGGERS CLUB (where goal oriented women help each other, share ideas, read, travel, and invest) send an email to ILoveBaje@gmail.com

A Gold Digger's Guide

lenstalk@gmail.com (handwritten)

CPSIA information can be obtained at www.ICGtesting.com
Printed in the USA
BVOW071852130912

300394BV00001B/78/P

9 780615 248240